Marthe Robin

and the Foyers of Charity

By the same author

Marthe Robin, A Chosen Soul
with Fr Michel Tierny and David Fanning
CTS Biographies, B652

Marthe Robin
and the Foyers
of Charity

Martin Blake

Martin Blake

Theotokos Books

Published by Theotokos Books
Nottingham, England

www.theotokos.org.uk
books@theotokos.org.uk

First Published in 2010

Cover art by Anthony Connolly

Cover design/implemenation by Mike Daley

ISBN 978-0955074622

Contents

Acknowledgements

I should like to acknowledge and thank here all those who have led me to know about Marthe, and those who have helped me in writing this book. There were Robert and Margaret Hansford who first lent me *The Cross and the Joy*, the first book in English about Marthe Robin, and with whom I visited Châteauneuf twice. There was Père Michel Tierny who welcomed me to his Foyer at Courset, near Boulogne, for my first Retreat in 1984, and which I have revisited several times. His little book on Marthe is included in the CTS booklet, *Marthe Robin: A Chosen Soul*. I would also mention Archbishop Mario Conti of Glasgow, who as Bishop of Aberdeen was an early enthusiast for a Foyer in the U.K.

Above all, I wish to thank Donal Foley, (to whom this book is dedicated), whom I first met on a Hansford Walking Pilgrimage to Fatima in 1986, and who has been my chief collaborator in working for a Foyer in the UK. Together we founded the "English Friends of the Foyers," and organised a series of Foyer-type retreats from 1997 to 2004. Not only has he both read and edited this book, but he has published it through Theotokos Books.

The English Friends produce a newsletter giving details of Foyer Retreats and other relevant information usually twice a year. To receive a copy by post, or the electronic version, please see the section containing further information at the end of this book.

There are the several priests who conducted our Foyer-type retreats, and supported us in the early days, to whom we are very grateful. More recently there are Fr David Hartley and

Mgr Keith Barltrop who have emerged providentially to develop the Foyer movement still further, and are now our main clerical supporters. Mgr Keith has also been most encouraging over the writing of this book, for which he has written the Foreword. Thanks, also, to Stratford Caldecott for his Preface.

May I thank, too, Lynne Hunter-Johnson who has read this book as it progressed, and also Philip Trower, Antony Tyler and Alistair Ozanne for their encouragement. Thanks, too, to Cecilia Scovil, of La Part Dieu Foyer near Paris, the only English Foyer Member so far; and to Dom Philippe Jobert OSB, the monk of Solesmes who led me into the Church in the mid-fifties, and has kept me "on the straight and narrow" for more than half a century with his sound advice; he too is a great supporter of Marthe.

Thanks also to Fergal Martin of the Catholic Truth Society for permission to use material from the CTS booklet on Marthe.

Finally, special thanks to Leo Madigan and Francis Phillips for their wise suggestions, to Père Raymond Peyret for his four biographies which have been so useful, and to Anthony Connolly for his cover picture of Marthe. Special thanks to Béatrice Soulary for permission to use the picture of the divan bed in Marthe's room found on the back cover.

Foreword

Marthe Robin was one of the most extraordinary and influential figures, not just of the twentieth century Church, but of all time. Yet she is but little-known in the English-speaking world. This is a great loss to us, because her teaching, like that of St Thérèse of Lisieux, whose spiritual daughter she is, conveys an authentic word of God for our time, and one of capital importance. Indeed, her whole life, such a long one in contrast with that of St Thérèse, is a word of God to us, as can be seen from the huge number of people she influenced, both personal visitors, those with whom she corresponded, and those who have simply read about her or visited "La Plaine," near Châteauneuf-de-Galaure, since her death.

Martin Blake is therefore to be warmly thanked and congratulated on writing this informative and highly readable biography of Marthe for English-speaking readers. It is truly a ground-breaking work, and full of the insights Martin has accumulated over his own long life. I particularly appreciate the way he is able to relate her life and teaching to spiritual reference points with which readers will be more familiar.

Among the many new movements and communities in the Church of today with whose birth and growth she was intimately connected, one stands out, the great work Our Lord himself entrusted to her and Fr Finet: the Foyers of Charity. These, too, are but little known in the English-speaking world, though increasing numbers of people have been on a Foyer retreat and, having experienced its fruits, are wondering when a Foyer can be established in Britain.

Marthe has rightly been hailed as one of the prophets of the Second Vatican Council, yet it is being realised that for the Council's vision of a new Pentecost to be fulfilled, communities such as the Foyers are essential. They have a unique role to play in forming the lay apostles, as Marthe would have said, or evangelists—as we might say today—that our world needs more than ever.

My prayer is that Martin's book will serve both to make more Catholics aware of the great gift Marthe Robin is to the Church of today, and to help prepare for the great day when a Foyer of Charity will be founded in Britain.

Mgr Keith Barltrop - Former Director of CASE, the Catholic Agency to Support Evangelisation

Preface

The Foyers de Charité were founded in 1936 by Marthe Robin and her spiritual director, Fr Georges Finet. Like St. Thérèse of Lisieux and Cardinal Newman, Marthe was a prophetic soul who, decades before the Second Vatican Council, foresaw the need for an active and effective lay apostolate in the coming century, an apostolate which would deal specifically with the needs of our modern world.

The response of Marthe and Fr Finet was to set up a "Foyer"—literally, a "hearth" or a place of welcome—where people could come on retreat and be filled with the goodness and love of God, mediated to them through the sacraments, prayer, and a gentle, very Marian and motherly witness, by those members who have devoted their lives to God. The revolutionary thing about the Foyers was the collaboration between the lay people running the Foyer, and the priest who dedicated himself, with the full support of his bishop, as the spiritual Father of the community.

The initial Foyer at Châteauneuf-de-Galaure, where Marthe lived, gave rise to other such "centres of light, love and charity," first in France, and eventually all over the world. At present there are more than seventy Foyers, and the movement has been approved by the Pontifical Council for the Laity. Apart from countries in both Western and Eastern Europe, many of these are in Africa and Asia; three are in Canada, one in the USA and one in Mexico, while there are nearly a dozen in South America and the Caribbean. Thus the Foyers are part of a world-wide evangelising mission.

There is a crying need for holiness, among both clergy and laity, a holiness which takes the example of Christ himself as its source, and it seems to me that it would be most helpful to have such "centres of holiness" in this country.

Marthe Robin was one of the great mystical figures of the modern Church, and the movement she founded has already borne much fruit. Martin Blake's careful study is a tribute to this great figure and a contribution to the renewal of tradition that Catholics have longed for since the Second Vatican Council.

Stratford Caldecott - Editor, *Second Spring*

Introduction

In 1982, I was lent *The Cross and the Joy* by Père Raymond Peyret, and discovered Marthe Robin. Over a quarter of a century later, it remains the only book in English about this remarkable French mystic, and it is a translation from French. Since then I have devoted quite a lot of time and energy to propagating the story of Marthe and the Foyers, in the hope that one day a Foyer of Charity might be established in the United Kingdom. I have read almost everything published about her, in French, and have visited Foyers in three continents. On many occasions I have been on Foyer Retreats.

In recent years there has been a spate of new biographies about Marthe. In 2006 came a life written by the Postulator of her Cause, Père Bernard Peyrous. Then came a fourth book by her original biographer Père Raymond Peyret, and finally, in 2008, a book by Père Jacques Ravanel who was the successor to Père Finet, the co-founder of the Foyers, and Marthe's first Postulator. This biographical activity has convinced me, at last, that what Anglophones need is an original study by an Englishman; and so I have been galvanised into action.

I have tried to be as objective and fair as possible, while recognising that Marthe is still the subject of controversy. That she is one of the most important figures in twentieth century Catholicism I have no doubt. Nor do I doubt that the Foyer movement will be of increasing importance in the twenty-first century. But the fact that it has almost entirely failed to penetrate the Anglophone parts of the world seems to me significant, and it is my hope that this study may help to correct this. For, like it or not, there is little doubt that English is the world language of the future; and the influence of Marthe and the Foyers, like all things Catholic, is for the whole world.

So this is the first book on Marthe Robin written in English by an English person, and I very much hope that it may be a worthy successor to the CTS Booklet, (B 652), that was published in 1999. May it serve to bring her astonishing life to the notice of an increasing number of English-speaking Catholics all over the world, and to encourage the foundation of new Foyers of Charity.

All history is subjective to a certain extent. The author has to select the "facts" he wishes to present and to interpret them. Even the so-called facts may be open to question; one has only to ask two or three people who witnessed an event to describe it to get quite a varied picture of what happened. Hard-line dictatorships interpret history to suit their purposes; examples of this were common well before Marxist-Leninist days. For example, Dr Edwin Jones has drawn attention to the way in which Henry VIII's henchmen wrote preambles to the Acts of 1533 and 1534 which abolished appeals to Rome and then proclaimed the King as "Head of the Church of England", which gave an entirely new slant to medieval history. Professor Butterworth called the myth about the "Reformation" that was taught to English youth, the "Whig Interpretation of History".

In the same way biography can be more subjective that objective. And in the case of hagiographical studies extreme care has to be observed. Thus I have embarked on a study of a modern French mystic with some trepidation. Jean Guitton, the distinguished French philosopher, wrote of Marthe Robin that "she was the most remarkable character of the twentieth century". Many have noted with regret that her spiritual director, Fr Finet, did not leave more reminiscences of his forty-five years in company with Marthe. But we have plenty of others, like Guitton and Marcel Clément, who subsequently wrote with vivid pens, as did Père Marie-Dominique Philippe OP. I have drawn particularly on these three, since they all knew Marthe intimately over a long period.

Foyers have quietly been established in every continent over the last seventy years, and they are especially sought after by bishops in Africa, a continent that has only really been Christianised for little over a century. It is there, and in Asia, that the Church is growing so strongly.

One may wonder why Marthe's Cause for beatification has not advanced more swiftly, but doubtless this is what a Benedictine friend calls, "Le secret de Dieu". I cannot believe it can be delayed much longer, and I hope this little book will help her Cause in the Anglophone world.

Prologue

On 10 February 1936, Fr Georges Finet, a young Priest in his thirties, drove from the city of Lyon, in south-eastern France, to the village of Châteauneuf-de-Galaure in the Drôme foothills, to visit Marthe Robin. In his car he had a hand-coloured picture of Mary Mediatrix of all Graces, which he had been asked to deliver personally to Marthe, who lived with her parents in a small farmhouse a mile from the village.

She was the youngest of six children, born in 1902, and had been bedridden since 1928, and from 1929 more or less paralyzed. She had a reputation for an intense prayer life and a very deep union with Christ and His Mother; in October 1930 she had been marked with the stigmata of His Passion and every Friday she underwent the Passion of Christ.

This providential meeting led to a partnership between Fr Finet and Marthe which would only be broken by her death in 1981, by which time some sixty Foyers of Charity had been established on five continents; and since then even more communities have been founded.

During three hours of conversation the Abbé Finet was convinced by Marthe that his vocation lay in helping her. They spoke for the first hour about the Blessed Virgin and her role in the Church, and Fr Finet, who gave Marian conferences on the teaching of St Louis de Montfort, was astonished at the depth of her insights.

Then Marthe began to talk of the great events which were soon to occur in the world, some rich in graces—usually taken as a reference to the Second Vatican Council—and others very painful, presumably a reference to World War II. Marthe then spoke of a renewal of the Church by means of the laity and a "New Pentecost of Love," which would take many forms, but outstanding in this process would be new communities, the Foyers, "Homes" of Light, Charity and Love.

These communities were to be made up of consecrated lay persons and directed by a Priest, the Father of the Foyer; Marthe saw their main task as providing week-long silent retreats to be given by him. She maintained that the Foyers would have a worldwide influence, and would particularly be "an expression of the Heart of Jesus to the nations after the defeat of materialism and satanic errors." Amongst these she mentioned Communism and Freemasonry.

Following this, Marthe asked Fr Finet to come to Châteauneuf to found the first Foyer of Charity, telling him that this was the express wish of God. She also told him that he would be required to preach retreats, to be held in silence, initially for women and girls, and that the first of these was to take place the following September. She reassured him that the Blessed Virgin would take care of everything to do with publicity and the necessary finance.

He said he was willing but would have to ask permission from his superiors. These subsequently agreed to this request as did his spiritual director, a professor of theology, who was enthusiastic about the idea since he had already met Marthe. Thus thirty-three persons, all women, assembled seven months later for the first retreat, and indeed two of these would eventually become permanent members of the first Foyer.

1

Marthe Robin's Early
Life: 1902–1925

When St Thérèse of the Child Jesus and the Holy Face, O.Carm., died of tuberculosis at the age of twenty-four in the Carmel at Lisieux in 1897, nobody could have imagined that within a quarter of a century the Church would beatify her, and go on to proclaim her a saint in 1925. Nor would they have imagined that her autobiography, *The Story of a Soul*, would be read by millions of Catholics in many languages, or that Pope Pius X would call her "the greatest saint of modern times". Since then she has been proclaimed Patroness of the Missions, and more recently a Doctor of the Church. There is more than a touch of God in all this, a definite intervention of the supernatural.

In the same way one can only explain the life and influence of the French mystic Marthe Robin in terms of the supernatural. From time to time, God raises up someone in the Church quite unexpectedly to reveal his power, and to influence those who are led into contact with that person. Such in the twentieth century were Saints Faustina and Pio, in Poland and Italy, Mother Teresa in India, and Thérèse and Marthe in France, as well as the seers of the apparitions of Our Lady approved by the Church.

There was quite a close connection between Thérèse and Marthe, as we shall see. Marthe was drawn to the Carmelite life as she entered her twenties, but this hope was frustrated by growing illness. However, in 1925 she received mystical visits from Thérèse on three occasions, and these had a profound effect on her.

Marthe's Early Life

So, who was Marthe Robin, and what was her influence in the Church? Marthe was born in March 1902, the youngest child of six, into a modest farming family who had a smallholding about a mile from the village of Châteauneuf-de-Galaure, near the Rhone Valley south of Lyon. It was the year that St Maria Goretti was murdered by Alessandro Serenelli. Sometimes described as "peasants," though that term would soon be as dated as the medieval "serf," the Robins owned some ten hectares of land and a solid farmhouse on the plateau above the village, from where on a clear day there was an extraordinary view in all directions, including the Alps. They were not exactly poor, nor in any sense rich, but they were independent and made a reasonable living from crops and livestock by working hard.

The district in the Drôme Department suffered, as did so much of France, from declining religious practise and a rise in belief in socialism and its corollary, anti-clericalism. The political climate was republican and freemasonic, and the persecution at the turn of the century, with the separation of Church and State, and the hostile Acts of Association that drove so many Catholic communities into exile—many to England—affected the region considerably.

The Robin family were Catholic, if not particularly religious, and Marthe was baptised by the Abbé Caillet three weeks after her birth, on Holy Saturday. Her brother Henri, aged twelve, was her godfather. A year later there was an outbreak of typhoid fever in the district and the sister above her named Clémence died at the age of five. Both Alice, the one above that, and Marthe were weakened by the disease, but survived. In 1905, the teaching sisters were expelled, and the village school was staffed by the secular state.

School and Religious Development

At the age of six, Marthe joined her sisters and other children from Moïlles, as the area on the plateau was called, at the village school, which entailed a two kilometre walk morning and evening. She seems to have been perfectly happy in the school, and got on well with her teachers. That same year her eldest sister Célina married and settled nearby. Marthe missed Célina, but as she grew older she often visited her, particularly when her husband was called to fight in the First World War. From what little evidence we have it seems that Marthe was a normal child, sometimes mischievous, but who not infrequently missed days at school on account of illness; she eventually left without any "certificat d'études."

As for religious formation, it is not clear whether she received this at Châteauneuf or nearby Saint-Bonnet. What we do know is that the catechism book from which she was instructed was dull in the extreme. As was normal right up to Vatican II, children had to learn the answers to formal questions by heart. For example: "What is the Apostles' Creed?" "The Apostles' Creed is the profession of faith which comes to us from the Apostles." "How many articles of faith does it contain?" "There are twelve articles which are truths we are bound to believe." And so on...! Marthe did not warm to this kind of instruction, and was later heard to comment: "There was no love in that catechism."

However she liked the teacher, who was able to enthuse her pupils with the Faith, and taught them to pray. And the Holy Spirit, who is the principal catechist, led her to a knowledge and love of Jesus Christ. As for the second commandment "to love one's neighbour", there were plenty of practical examples at La Plaine, where Mme Robin often gave simple food to wandering beggars. And she also encouraged her children to share their treats with less well-off people.

We are told that from the age of five, Thérèse Martin began to show an interest in spiritual practices, such as visits to the Blessed Sacrament with her father. In Marthe's case we have this reminiscence: "My sisters didn't want me praying all the time, so I prayed chiefly in bed. I would pray to the Blessed Virgin and talk with her. I used prayers that I found in my grandfather's prayer book. When I walked down to the village I always carried my rosary in my pocket and prayed as I went along."

In May 1911 she received the sacrament of Confirmation, and made her First Communion on the Feast of the Assumption 1912. "I think Our Lord took possession of me then", she was to write in due course. Two years later, as the war clouds were gathering, she made what was called a "Solemn Communion" with other children. That year war broke out with Germany, a war which was to gravely weaken France for a generation or more. Thus at the age of twelve her formal education was complete, and she began to help her parents on the farm. Later she would write: "The prayer of children is very powerful with the Heart of God. Pray often with them, and lead them to love prayer. It is by means of the child that the family will grow in faith."

Marthe's Health Declines

Working on the little farm at La Plaine, she shared in some ways the experience of the three young shepherds at Fatima at the same time. Their's may have been a more expansive life—they covered surprising distances with their sheep—but both loved their time with animals in the open air. And both delighted in prayer. There was, however, no angel or private revelation of Our Lady in Marthe's youth, and God was to form a relationship with her in a somewhat different way. Like Jacinta she loved to laugh and dance. And like her she was introduced to suffering through illness, but she was not destined to die young. Like the Fatima children, Marthe advanced along the way of holiness.

It was in 1918, a year after the Miracle of the Sun at Fatima, that Marthe's health began to decline. She suffered severe headaches, and consulted a doctor at Saint-Sorlin. She developed fainting fits, and about the time of the Armistice— St Martin's Day—she fell in the kitchen and couldn't get up. Other doctors were consulted, and one suggested she might have a brain tumour. There were other indications of what was to come: partial paralysis and weakness of the eyes.

One day, during a visit from the parish priest, Abbé Payre, she fell asleep, and several months later woke up and immediately asked for the priest, taking up the conversation where she had left off. It may be that Marthe suffered from a form of encephalitis during this time, a coma of some sort, which lasted for approximately seventeen months, although she was not always unconscious. She remained in bed until 1921. That May she experienced her first vision of the Blessed Virgin. She shared this with her sister Alice who slept in the same room, although Alice saw only a bright light after hearing a loud noise: Marthe said, "Yes, the light is beautiful, but I also saw the Blessed Virgin."

Her health appeared to improve a little that summer, and she was able to do needlework and read. She became an avid reader, and her sisters supplied her with books from the parish library. She could also write, and began to fill notebooks with copied poems and spiritual texts. There was much talk at that time of Thérèse Martin the young Carmelite who had died in 1897, whose autobiography was being widely read, and who was to be beatified by Pius XI in 1923. Marthe sometimes thought she would like to try her vocation to Carmel, but of course her fragile health precluded this.

Marthe Discovers her Vocation

In the spring of 1922 she went to keep house for her sister Gabrielle who had to be away for a few days in Marseille. She looked after Gabrielle's child and her grandfather. It was during that visit that she found her way up to the attic, where in an old trunk she examined some ancient books. Thumbing through one of them she came across the following: "Why search for peace when you are destined to struggle? Why look for pleasure when you are made for suffering?" And apparently she remarked to herself: "For you there will be suffering!" This prophecy was to be well and truly fulfilled. Another saying she recalled from the book was: "One must give God everything."

There has been some speculation as to what the book she found in the attic was. Some think it might have been *The Imitation of Christ*. Or it could have been *The Secret of Mary* by St Louis-Marie de Montfort. Yet another suggestion is the *Letter to the Friends of the Cross* composed in 1714 by the same author. Certainly this great Marian saint, whose works, oddly enough, were hidden for over a hundred years in a chest, was to play a big part in her life in due course.

Back at La Plaine, Marthe was again faced with the cross of her illness, a cross not easy to bear with joy. As 1922 progressed she developed pains in her back, her eyes and her teeth. She took to wearing glasses. By the autumn she was again using crutches. It was the following year that a doctor suggested she go to Saint-Péray, on the other side of the Rhone opposite Valence, where rheumatics were treated with hot and cold baths. She underwent various treatments for three weeks without evident improvement. She was just twenty-one. It was there she was befriended by a baroness called Madame du Bay, who lived not far from Châteauneuf, and who often came to visit her thereafter. She was a devout lady with a good religious library. Marthe was still torn between giving all to God and hoping for a normal life. It was the priest of Saint-Uze who recalled her saying: "I struggled with God!" The years 1923 to 1925 were filled with anguish.

In August of 1923 the Abbé Faure took over the parish of Châteauneuf. To start with, and for some time, he and Marthe did not hit it off. Had he not prayed as a seminarian to be spared mystic women?

A graphologist was later shown some of Marthe's letters written at this time and made some revealing comments on her psychological evolution between 1923 to 1925, which Raymond Peyret quotes in his book published in 2007. By 1925 she had come to accept that God had a mission for her in her handicap and illness. That summer, Fr Faure obtained a place for her on a diocesan pilgrimage to Lourdes, but when she heard about another sick woman in a neighbouring village who was keen to go, and there was no more room, she gave up her place in her favour, to Fr Faure's incomprehension. This was a considerable sacrifice of love, and a turning-point in her spiritual life. Out Lady was going to obtain a host of graces for Marthe, but they would not include a physical cure. She was now ready to consecrate her life to Christ.

Portrait of Marthe in 1925

This year was an important one in Marthe's spiritual journey. So let us pause and try to throw some light on the state of her life then. She was twenty-three and already fairly handicapped by illness. She had made four friends locally who were to play a role in her subsequent life. There was Gisèle Bouteville who used to come to Châteauneuf on holiday from Lyon and met Marthe in 1924. Five years later she married Monsieur Signé, and has left interesting memoirs of Marthe. Another was Jeanne Bonneton whose family lived locally. She got to know Marthe a few years later, and for a while helped her as a secretary; she eventually found her vocation as a Poor Clare and finished up as Abbess of her community. Paulette Plantevin was a friend of Abbé Faure, and visited Marthe regularly from 1926 to 1930; she too acted as her secretary. Finally there was Marguerite Lautru, a convert from an anti-clerical family, who planned to become a religious even before receiving baptism. She practised as a midwife at Châteauneuf from 1925 to 1927 before joining the Sisters of

Charity in Lyon where she eventually became Mother General. All four women have thrown useful light on Marthe during this period.

Marthe's Friends and Visitors

Marguerite Lautru was probably Marthe's closest friend, with whom she had most in common; she was a frequent visitor at this important time. Not all Marthe's contemporaries in the village spoke well of her; some feared contagion and some thought she was a fraud. At times Marthe felt quite lonely, and she valued visits from her few good friends all the more. She had been at the village school, and was known to most of the locals. But we must not exaggerate; La Plaine was after all a good mile out of the village, and probably few young people are good at "visiting the sick" or any other of the Church's "corporal works of mercy". Gisèle Signé noted that Marthe never looked in good health, though she smiled a lot, and was very grateful to receive visitors. Marthe's mother never gave up in her duties towards her sick daughter, but it seems that her father became more than a little fed up at times.

Praying, reading and needlework filled her days. To try and pay for her medication, mainly aspirin, and occasional visits from a doctor, she sold prettily embroidered work and knitted garments via a Mlle Caillet. But Marthe also loved giving things away as presents; and to raise a little money for charities and the missions she also dealt in unwanted items such as barometers. She loved to give her friends refreshments when they came to see her, and would prepare cream cakes and jam. She would be sitting in the kitchen to receive her visitors; she was always reticent to discuss her illness and troubles, but showed great interest in the lives and doings of her friends and family. Marguerite Lautru says that humility was her hallmark.

Then, and for the rest of her life, she had an extraordinary capacity for friendship and interest in whoever happened to be with her. The pattern of her dealings with the estimated hundred thousand visitors who were to see her during the next fifty years was already evident. Marguerite records that they sometimes sang together and also prayed; St Thérèse often came into their conversation. Paulette Plantevin recalls being a little frightened when Marthe spoke of the devil, and Gisèle noted how beautifully she spoke and wrote about "le Bon Dieu".

Marthe's Acts of Abandonment

In 1930 Marthe wrote: "I dared to choose Jesus Christ. One day, having consecrated myself to Him and received clear proof that my humble act of Abandonment had been accepted, He revealed himself to me and gave himself spiritually to me as the spouse of my soul, living and active."

Just two months after giving up her place on the pilgrimage to Lourdes, she experienced a wonderful interior sense of calm and peace which made her want to live entirely for God. It was on 15 October 1925, the feast of St Teresa of Avila, and not long after Pope Pius XI had canonised St Thérèse of Lisieux, that Marthe composed her first Act of Abandonment. Such documents are not infrequent in Church history. St Thérèse had composed one in 1895. The theology of the nineteenth century tended to emphasise the notion of sacrifice to propitiate the Justice of God. What was new in St Thérèse's theology was an emphasis on Love. The other noticeable shift in both Thérèse and Marthe is that they are not really giving anything to God—they are rather accepting whatever He will send them. "Take my life, Lord." The other model for Marthe's Act was one made by a Père Bouchard which had come to her notice.

Believing that she was not destined to remain long in this world, Marthe decided to destroy the first version, which apparently she kept hidden under her pillow; but this was not before she had shown it to Abbé Faure who made a copy to give to Abbé Perrier of Saint-Uze, which is now in the possession of one of Marthe's nieces. Eighteen months later,

Marthe wrote a second version, considerably developed and amplified. In this second Act she uses the term "je me livre" rather than "give or abandon"; and this notion she develops, as we shall see. Another characteristic of the second Act is the idea that her sacrifice may help millions of other people, sinners and those who have wandered from the truth, culpably or in ignorance. Finally there is a Marian dimension in the second Act. Mary was hardly mentioned in the first, but she receives a whole section at the end of the second Act of Abandonment. Thus Marthe renounces her own will completely, and is ready to accept whatever God has in store for her. She was now entirely open to the work of the Holy Spirit.

This second act begins as follows:
"I hand my life to You in self-abandonment. Eternal God, Infinite Love! O my Father, you have asked your little victim to give everything. So, take and receive all ... this day I give and consecrate myself to You, wholly and with no turning back. .."

This remarkable document makes it clear that from now on Marthe is no longer in control of her life. It is the Lord who will now direct it. From now on Marthe will die to herself and be entirely guided by the Holy Spirit.

2

Marthe Robin: 1925–1930

This period following her Acts of Abandonment was marked
by declining health and increasing consciousness of her
vocation. The years 1926 to 1928 were very difficult. For a
start eating became more and more of a problem, and the
various doctors consulted could offer no solution. Marthe was
convinced she was dying, and for the second time she
received the "last sacraments", brought to her this time by
Abbé Faure. It was then that she claimed to have received
mystic visits on three occasions from her heroine Thérèse of
Lisieux. According to Marthe, the Carmelite saint assured her
she would not die but would carry on her mission to the wider
world. Later Marthe was to joke with Père Finet in the words:
"Ah, the rascal! She left everything to me." These mystical
interventions would have occurred during the winter of 1926-
27, and indeed there was a slight improvement in her health
early in 1927.

On 2 March she wrote in her journal: "I have been better
for some days and can remain out of bed for most of the day.
But I can think and do little. And my devoted mother has to
help me with my slightest movements, though I do retain the
use of my arms and hands to a certain extent. Yet I thank the
Good God for all that He gives me, and particularly for the
use of my hands which allows me to offer slight service on
behalf of my dear parents. Oh, that I may always be of use

with Him and for Him alone!" Marthe may have been disorientated but she was undoubtedly keeping up her abandonment to the will of God.

The Dominican theologian Père Manteau-Bonamy, who studied under the celebrated Garrigou-Lagrange, who also came to meet Marthe, made a study of her writings shortly before his regrettably early death, and wrote two books which throw much light on Marthe's thought at this time, *Marthe Robin sous la Conduite de Marie 1925-1932*, (1995), and *Prier 15 Jours avec Marthe Robin*, (1999). It was to him that Marthe said at their first meeting in 1945: "Just as Mary said to Bernadette 'I am the Immaculate Conception', so in regard to her being the Mother of God should we not call her 'The Divine Maternity.' " This, he said, helped him with his work on Mary published in 1949 entitled *Maternité Divine et Incarnation*.

Marthe Suffers during 1927

In March 1927, Marthe also wrote: "I am experiencing how sweet it is to love even while suffering; for suffering is the incomparable school of real love. It is the living language of love and the great educator of the human race. One learns to love chiefly through suffering, for real suffering leads us away from human delights to renunciation of oneself on the Cross." Most of us find such words difficult to grasp, but for Marthe, restricted as she was by her handicapped body, they provide a link with what St Thérèse wrote in one of her letters: "Let us not believe that we can love without suffering, and suffering a lot. That is part of our poor nature!" And of course it unites us with the redemptive suffering of Christ. This was what St Paul called "the folly of the Cross". Again, Marthe wrote about this time: "Christ accepted the suffering of the Cross willingly, and He proposed it to his followers as the only way to holiness and salvation, when He said: 'If anyone wishes to come after me, let him renounce himself, take up his cross and follow me.' " It certainly remains one of the most perplexing aspects of Catholic theology, that Christ had to suffer so grievously in his Passion, and that someone like Marthe was called to share that suffering for more than half a century.

Here is one more quotation from Marthe written in May 1927. "Alleluia! Alleluia! At last I can love Him with my whole heart, love Him without measure, my Saviour and my God truly present and living in me! I am no longer afraid of all his loving graces, of all his many marks of tenderness in these last times. I swim in thanksgiving and in the love of a child of God! My troubles, my fears, even my weaknesses and incapacity to be useful for anything, all that has disappeared or has become easy for me to bear, since I have had the immense joy of receiving Communion alongside my dear mother." This shows how much the Eucharist meant to her.

The Paralysis of her legs becomes definitive

From a letter she wrote to her chemist in July asking for more aspirin we can gather something of the extent of her daily, and nightly, suffering. Severe toothache was added to her other pains, and the local dentist had to extract several of her teeth. In March 1928 the paralysis of her legs became definitive, and she could no longer get up from her bed. It was in July that she ordered the divan on which she was to spend the remaining fifty-three years of her life, and where she would neither eat, drink or sleep; it was shorter than a bed, since her legs were folded back. She lived in a room which opened off the kitchen on the front of the house. She could still move her arms and hands, but she would never walk again. Marthe was well aware that her parents were ageing, and found caring for her increasingly difficult. Her visitors became rarer, and even the parish priest, Abbé Faure, was discouraged from coming to see her because her brother Henri took exception to his visits.

In late 1928 there occurred an event which was to be crucial in Marthe's spiritual progress. Two Capuchin friars were invited by Abbé Faure to lead a mission to the parish, and Fr Marie-Bernard and Fr Jean came for a whole month. Gisèle Signé recalls their visit to La Plaine. Fr Marie-Bernard remarked to Abbé Faure: "You have a saint up at Moïlles that you are unaware of!" This seems to have been the first time the word "saint" was used in connection with Marthe. The missioner had published a book on St Thérèse, so he was qualified to judge. He advised Marthe to read only books on spirituality, reported Gisèle. He also invited her to become a Tertiary, in other words a member of the Third Order of St Francis, for lay people, and the ceremony took place on 2 November. She was specially dressed for the occasion, and photographs were taken.

Christ, Our Lady and the devil ...

Abbé Faure wrote in his journal that on the night of 4 December, Our Lord appeared to Marthe and asked her if she would be willing to suffer for the conversion of sinners in general and for the parish in particular. Christ also asked her to accept Fr Faure as her spiritual director. So, from that day there was an entirely fresh relationship between Marthe and Fr Faure, which was to last for the next seven years. Marthe was as usual reticent about this episode, but it does seem to have been a turning-point in her life. "You see Gisèle, I have a fresh direction to my life." On 16 December, Marthe wrote a letter to Fr Faure asking him to be her spiritual father, which he kept in his wallet until his death.

There is incontestable evidence at this time both of confrontations with the devil, who notoriously hates holy people, and of apparitions of Our Lady, who notoriously opposes the serpent. For example, Jeanne Bonneton affirms that the devil broke two of Marthe's teeth the night after she became a Franciscan Tertiary in 1928, when she suddenly let out a cry. Suffice it to say that the attacks of the fallen angel continued throughout her life, as did the support given her by the Immaculate Conception.

Another priest who helped Marthe at this juncture was Père Betton, who was sent to see her by the Bishop of Valence, Mgr Pic. He was a professor of philosophy and theology in the diocesan seminary, and a friend of Abbé Perrier. He became for a while another of her spiritual directors. He always spoke warmly of her, and is quoted as saying: "I felt the presence of God when with her."

Marthe becomes progressively more Paralysed

In February 1929, Marthe felt her arms becoming paralysed like her legs, and she was no longer able to write or embroider. From now on she never ate or drank or slept. She was entirely handicapped physically, yet she retained her mental balance to an astonishing degree. She could pray and talk, dictate letters and thoughts, and still enjoy visitors. Abbé Faure came frequently, (we do not know how Henri took this), and encouraged her to dictate her prayers and even two remarkable poems, which are typical examples of French classical verse.

The first, written on New Years Day 1930, consisted of 18 lines of rhyming hexameters which would not be out of place in a collection of nineteenth-century verse, and the second, written in February 1930, was of four verses of four lines each in the same meter. Both are beautifully crafted. The second verse begins: "Je suis ta proie, O Jesus, dans la croix et la joie ... Dans la cruelle épreuve et la vive douleur." From these lines Père Peyret derived the title for the very first biography of Marthe called La Croix et La Joie, which he wrote the year she died, (1981), and which was translated into fifteen languages.

In March 1930, she was dictating: "My heart overflows with love and peace in God." One might imagine she was no longer suffering! But she added: "It is joy in the most complete sacrifice." By April she was writing of a dark night in her soul, and she wrote to Jeanne Bonneton, who had just become a Poor Clare, "Pray that those around me do not see how much I suffer." The gold was being purified by fire.

The Stigmata

The five years from 1925 to 1930 had utterly transformed Marthe both physically and spiritually. She was now like clay in the hand of the Potter, ready to be prepared for her great vocation. Like the body of St Francis of Assisi, her body too was to be marked by the signs of their Master's Passion. At the end of September, Jesus appeared to her and asked her: "Do you want to be like Me?" Five years before she had abandoned herself entirely to his will. Now He asked her for the supreme sacrifice. We are told that, as with St Francis, darts of fire sprang from Jesus' Heart and pierced her hands and feet. She felt herself stretched upon his Cross. A third dart pierced her side leaving a mark ten centimetres in length. Blood began to flow. At the same time Jesus pressed his crown of thorns onto her head. From then on her tears became bloodstained. When at her death the stigmata largely disappeared, the marks on her forehead remained. From 1931 she began her weekly experience of Our Lord's Passion, during which her wounds sometimes bled. Most of the stigmata were only apparent to her family and those who had to wash her clothes and sheets, but many thousands of her later visitors bore witness to the marks of the crown of thorns.

Medical Tests

In 1942, Mgr Pic, her bishop, arranged for two doctors from Lyon to examine her clinically, and they attested to seeing the stigmata. Eleven years later, a well-known psychiatrist, Dr Alain Assailly, was asked by Père Finet to examine Marthe and he wrote a full report. In his old age he published a whole book on her medical condition, including the phenomenon of the stigmata, (*Marthe Robin, Témoignage d'un psychiatre*, Emmanuel, 1996), I have a signed copy. In it he devotes much space to arguing that Marthe could not in any way have suffered from what was called hysteria.

At one point he suggested that she might go for a while to a clinic to be observed more officially. She said that if her superiors wished it she would obey, but did he think it would really solve any problems? A good question ... no amount of medical observation or conjecture can explain this sort of mystical phenomenon. And it remained a mystery to Marthe herself who said later: "It is not for me or anyone else to understand the secrets of God. All I have to do is to adore, to accept, to bless and to abandon myself to Providence." The stigmata were a visible sign of God's approval of her offering and of her close link with the suffering of Christ on the Cross; but all her life she wished to remain hidden from the world, a humble child.

A remarkable analysis of the significance of the stigmata by Marthe herself, as recalled by Fr Finet, can be found on pages 109 and 110 of Père Peyret's book *L'Offrande d'une Vie,* (2007). Some examples of this are: "It is this union of love, which becomes light, that our Saviour reveals to the soul what He wants to do with it," and, "The soul has been carried so far that it can no longer turn back, nor does it wish to. It has no longer any wish than his; for a long time it has said to Him to do only what He wills."

Marthe's parents were naturally overwhelmed to see so much blood being shed by their daughter, but came to accept it as an act of God. Gisèle Signé was shown Marthe's bloodstained sheets and bedclothes. From this time until her death in 1981, Marthe experienced Our Lord's Passion every Friday, that is some 2,500 times. In the early days these phenomena ended on Friday evening; later they extended to Saturday, and finally in her last years right up to Monday morning. Many people witnessed them, and they were well documented by Fr Finet. From 1936 to 1948 she prayed aloud during her Passions; thereafter they took place in silence. Like her Master she suffered for the sins of humanity. A local woman from a neighbouring village is recorded as having said prophetically in 1930; "There is a great saint living at Châteauneuf. One day crowds will come to see her!"

Isaac Watts' Famous Hymn, (1707)

When I survey the wondrous Cross,
on which the Prince of Glory died,
My richest gain I count but loss,
and pour contempt on all my pride.

Forbid it Lord that I should boast,
save in the death of Christ, my God;
All the vain things that charm me most,
I sacrifice them to his blood.

See from his head, his hands,
his feet, sorrow and love flow mingled down;
Did e'er such love and sorrow meet,
or thorns compose so rich a crown?

Were the whole realm of nature mine,
that were an offering far too small;
Love so amazing, so divine,
demands my soul, my life, my all.

(I have included this well-known Anglican hymn here as it seems to relate so well to the themes in this chapter)

3

The Beginning of Marthe's
Mission: 1930–1936

The events of 1930 saw the start of Marthe's mission. One of her sayings was: "Take care over the departure! Holiness must come first ... the work will follow after." Five more years were to pass, however, before she met Père Finet and they inaugurated the first Foyer of Charity.

During the late twenties, Marguerite Lautru and Abbé Faure had started what was called a "patronage" in Châteauneuf. These were found all over France and their object was to form children in the Faith. Marthe was already pressing for a Catholic school to be established; but as usual lack of money prevented it. Abbé Perrier of Saint-Uze supported the idea, and he said to his colleague: "If Marthe asks you to do this, you must follow her instructions."

The First Foyer School

However, early in 1934 the old chateau at the top of the village came onto the market for a derisory sum. It had previously been used as a kind of night club, and had a fairly unsavoury reputation. Marthe wrote in her note-book: "I understood then, what I had not dared to hope, that it was in my own parish that the great work of God's Love, of which He had spoken to me so often, was to be achieved. It was to consist of the creation of a school for young children, which was to be the beginning of an even greater work." So, persuaded by Marthe, Abbé Faure bought the run-down chateau through one of his parishioners. The parish rallied round, and began the process of transforming the building into a school. In October, the first seven girls began their schooling there, two of whom were Marthe's nieces. Many people thought the whole scheme outrageous. But before long it was to become a highly-regarded boarding school for 400 girls of all ages.

Marthe's concern for children has become famous. She believed passionately in the power of the prayer of children. Here is a fine quotation from Marthe's subsequent writing. "Have not the hearts of children been created to pray and to love? How is it that so few pray? Yet the prayer of children is all-powerful. There is nothing finer that rises to God than the prayer of children. Several children united in prayer can achieve marvellous things. Oh mothers ... make your children love prayer! God will glorify you. Rest assured that the angels are praying along with your children." So this was to be the primary purpose of the new school, to lead the children to pray. By 1935 there were eighteen pupils, and five years later seventy. Marthe's work, inspired by God, was launched.

A Priest is Promised ...

For some years Marthe had been receiving messages from heaven that she was to look out for a priest who would come to her, take over from Abbé Faure, and found a Foyer of Light, Charity and Love. This message had been particularly strong in 1933, the nineteen-hundredth anniversary of the Death and Resurrection of Jesus Christ and the foundation of the Church. "He (the priest) will not be able to do anything without you or separated from you. I wish to transmit my orders to him via you, so that he may know my will. As time passes you will tell him everything that I ask. And you will not be able to do anything without him." Thus was the

ground laid for the crucial meeting in 1936 between Abbé
Finet and Marthe.

A Mme Lucien Gorse had been visiting Marthe from Lyon.
She spoke about her to a Mlle Blanck, who drove out to meet
Marthe in December 1935. To her, Marthe said how much
she would like a picture of the Blessed Virgin to place in the
new school. She would like it to be of Mary Mediatrix of all
Graces. Mlle Blanck replied that she thought she could lay
her hands on a nice engraving which she would have water-
coloured and sent to Marthe. When later she met Fr Faure, he
confided to her that he felt "out of his depth" with Marthe.
Back in Lyon she spoke with Mother Scatt at the Convent of
the Cenacle near the cathedral. It was she who suggested
asking Abbé Finet to deliver the picture. As Raymond Peyret
puts it: "Our Lady's trap was set."

The Meeting with Fr Finet – 10 February 1936

This was the day that Abbé Finet met Marthe and handed
over the picture of Mary Mediatrix of all Graces. In due
course we shall examine Fr Finet's background, but for the
moment let us simply follow his movements on that historic
day. He had not been to Châteauneuf before, but he had
heard about Marthe. So that morning he drove the fifty odd
miles from Lyon with the picture in the back of the car. At
about 11 o'clock he arrived at the presbytery and Abbé Faure
greeted him and went up with him to La Plaine. Mme Robin
was expecting them and settled them into the kitchen, where
M. Robin was ill—he was to die on 23 June. Faure went
through to Marthe's room, while Finet unwrapped the picture.
Then Faure reappeared and invited Finet to take the picture
into Marthe's room. Finet had a profound devotion to Our
Lady and indeed was well known in Lyon for his conferences
on the "True Devotion" of St Louis-Marie de Montfort. He
famously remarked later: "I thought I was bringing a picture of
the Blessed Virgin to Marthe, but in fact it was she who was
bringing me!" Marthe admired the picture, thanked Abbé

Finet, and asked him if he would like to come back after lunch. The two priests returned to the presbytery for the midday meal, and at 2 o'clock exactly Fr Finet called on Marthe for the second time. This visit lasted three hours.

Fr Finet retold the story many times; how for the first hour Marthe spoke largely of Our Lady, and how he was astonished by the depths of her insight. "They seemed to know each other rather well." Then she began to talk of the events that were soon to occur in the world, some very distressing, others rich in graces. It was then that she predicted a new Pentecost of Love which would be preceded by a renewal of the Church, in which the laity were to play an important part. They would be formed in many places, notably in Foyers of Light, Charity and Love. This prediction of a new Pentecost was to be echoed in due course by Popes Pius XII, John XXIII and Paul VI. When she said that the Church was to be renewed she may have been anticipating the Second Vatican Council.

Marthe explains the Foyers to Fr Finet

Abbé Finet asked her what she meant by "Foyers of Light, Charity and Love". They will be something quite new in the Church, she replied. They will consist of consecrated lay people, but not as in a religious order. They will be families headed by a priest, and with the Blessed Virgin as their mother. The teaching which will be given in the retreats conducted by the priest will be backed up by the whole community. The Foyers will spread throughout the world. They will be a response from the Heart of Jesus to the world after the satanic errors of so many. These would include Communism, secularism and Freemasonry. She foresaw an intervention on the part of Our Lady.

It was at 4 o'clock that Marthe addressed Abbé Finet with the words: "Monsieur l'Abbé, I have a request to make to you sent from God."

"What is that Mademoiselle?"

"It is you who must come here to Châteauneuf and found the first Foyer of Charity."

"Me? But I am not in this diocese. I am from Lyon."

"What matter, since God wishes it!"

"Ah, forgive me; but what shall I have to do?"

"Many things, notably to preach retreats."

"But I never have."

"You will learn!"

"I suppose three day retreats will be valuable."

"No, one cannot form a soul in three days. The Blessed Virgin asks for five whole days."

"I see; and who will attend these retreats?"

"To begin with ladies and older girls."

"How shall I occupy them? Workshops ... discussion groups?"

"No, Our Lady wants complete silence."

"Do you really think I shall be able to keep young ladies in silence for five days?"

"Yes, since that is what Our Lady requests."

"Ah, forgive me; I hadn't thought of it like that. But how shall we advertise these retreats?"

"The Blessed Virgin will see to that. Jesus will impart extraordinary graces. You will not need to advertise."

"And where will the retreats take place?"

"In the girls school here."

"But we shall need beds, and a kitchen. Who will do all the work?"

"You will!"

"And with what money?"

"Don't worry about that. Our Lady will see to it."

"When do you anticipate the first retreat?"

"Monday September 7th until the afternoon of Sunday 13th."

Abbé Finet thought a while and then said: "I cannot refuse. But I shall have to get permission from my superiors."

"Of course! You must remain under obedience."
Coming away from Marthe's room he was stunned. "What an
adventure!" he said to himself.

That evening Fr Faure went with Fr Finet to Lyon, and
both celebrated Mass in honour of Our Lady of Lourdes next
morning in the cathedral. He was in high spirits in the
knowledge that at last Marthe would have a fresh spiritual
director. Abbé Finet consulted his superior in the work for
Catholic schools, the Vicar General, and his confessor Père
Valensin SJ. All three encouraged him to take up Marthe's
challenge. The latter used prophetic words: "I have been to
see Marthe myself with the Bishop of Valence; we spent
several hours with her. She is like Catherine of Siena! She
will never mislead you. She is of the Church, and you will be
able to do whatever she tells you. Go ahead!" Mgr Pic of
Valence received him "with open arms". Only the
Archbishop was slightly reticent; he was loath to lose such a
good priest and he insisted that he continue to work at Lyon
part-time.

Georges Finet's Background

Lyon was the first Christian centre in Roman Gaul, and proud
of its ancient Catholic roots. In the nineteenth century it was
an early industrialised city, with a strong Christian presence,
despite being at the same time a centre of advanced socialist
thought. Georges' paternal grandparents were rooted in God.
His grandfather Pierre, who died in 1930, was a devotee of the
Rosary and composed the Prayer to St Joseph which was later
incorporated into the daily Foyer prayers. "I have often
thought that the numerous religious vocations among his
grand-children were due to his many rosaries," wrote a
grandchild. His business was as a wholesale supplier of goods
to the shops. Georges' mother was a Beaumont and came from
higher up the social scale in Lyon. The Beaumonts lived
comfortably in a suburb and were much involved in Church
activities.

So Georges grew up in a healthy Catholic family milieu. Of the thirteen children of his generation, siblings and cousins, half found vocations to serve the Church. His elder brother Pierre became a Jesuit while he became a secular priest, and one of his sisters became a nun. One of his uncles was killed in the war. Of his father Ludovic, (1864-1951), someone wrote: "He was straightforward, just, exact and thoughtful, a business man with his feet on the ground. Affable and warm-hearted, he was always kind and considerate of others." Georges' mother, Marie-Antoinette (1871-1949), was always elegantly turned out and believed in strict behaviour. "She was goodness personified" was how Georges described her. She kept open house for their many friends and relations, and also for the local clergy. Georges was the third of six children; his younger sister Genevieve married a surgeon and bore eight children, and his brothers Robert and Simon had nine and four respectively—a prolific family.

Fr Finet's Vocation

Born in 1898, he got on well with his siblings, and was to say later that he learnt about feminine purity from his sisters. He attended a religious boarding school, but had one day a week at home. There he was a good scholar and made some firm friends including the son of a leading industrial family, Alfred Ancel, who like him found his vocation to the priesthood. At the age of seventeen they both attended a retreat preached by a Mgr Saint-Clair, and both emerged certain that God was calling them to become priests. Since Georges' elder brother was already training to be a Jesuit, this was quite hard for their parents to accept, but they gave him every support. Later Fr Georges was to say: "Oh my children, when one has said 'yes' to God, what joy fills the heart! In my retreat notes I can feel an intense emotion of joy that filled my heart and soul. I think I can truthfully say that this joy has accompanied me during my whole life."

He was sent to the prestigious French College in Rome. It was there he discovered the *True Devotion to the Blessed Virgin* of St Louis de Montfort, which had a decisive influence on his life, as it was to have on that of John Paul II. In 1917, his training was interrupted by a call-up to military service, and he was commissioned as an artillery officer. This too was important for his formation. In 1919 he returned to Rome, where he was later present for the canonisation of St Joan of Arc and the beatification of St Thérèse of Lisieux.

The New Priest

He was ordained priest at Lyon in 1923 in company with his friend Alfred Ancel. "When a young priest goes for the first time into the intimacy of the confessional and hears a voice say 'Bless me father, for I have sinned', he is overwhelmed on hearing himself addressed as 'father' on account of his priesthood. This young man, who has left everything, who has renounced human paternity and the possibility of founding a family, now finds himself profoundly a father, deep in the intimacy of his heart. Little by little he sees all the joys and all the woes of the world, which come to his priesthood and cry out 'Abba, Father' ... And so at that moment a song of thanksgiving arises in the young man's heart, for just as he has renounced human paternity, he knows that in his priesthood he has made the discovery of divine paternity." Thus he recalled the greatness of the occasion in later years.

In 1924 he was appointed to the working-class parish of Oullins, but the following year the Archbishop transferred him to the cathedral staff, where he remained until 1934. During that time, Fr Finet toyed with the idea of a vocation to the religious life, but his Jesuit spiritual director, Fr Valensin, steered him towards an institute for secular priests called the "Society of the Heart of Jesus". Like the Anglo-Peruvian Fr Crawley-Boevey he developed a deep devotion to the Sacred Heart. For twenty years this society helped to sustain Georges Finet. At the same time he became something of a Marian expert, and he built up an extensive clientele to whom he gave conferences at the Convent of the Cenacle. In 1934 he was appointed assistant Director of Church Schools, responsible for some 800 independent schools. His superior was a future bishop.

A strange mystical event occurred in November 1930, when a mild earthquake caused damage on Fourvière Hill on which the cathedral stands. Fr Finet was out helping the victims when a wall collapsed nearly burying him. That night Marthe was made spiritually aware of the danger he was in, and suffered so much that Fr Faure had to be called. She told him of the earthquake before it was reported in the papers.

So when Abbé Finet met Marthe in February 1936, he was already a notable personality rich in experience. He was just four years older than Marthe. His time in the army, and later in the educational department, had developed his capacity to lead and direct. He was well-formed theologically and well-connected socially. Indeed he was the ideal priest to found the new Work of God.

France and the Church

Strangely enough, Marthe never recorded their meeting in her note-books, nor did she talk much about it subsequently. Our principal source of information is Fr Finet himself, corroborated by Mother Scatt in her personal diary, now in the Foyer archives. It was not, however, until February 1943 that he wrote a full account, which we have already quoted. Both Marthe and Fr Finet were strong believers in the important role that France had been given for the Church in the world, particularly since the Consecration to the Blessed Virgin made by Louis XIII in Chartres Cathedral in 1638. As a result, Our Lady of the Assumption was declared principal patroness of France, while 15 August was established as a national holiday. It was still the case that in the 1930s a majority of the Church's missionaries came from France, and despite anti-clerical republican governments the Church was strong. But the errors of the "Enlightenment" and the appalling massacre of World War I were seriously weakening the country, so that when John Paul II arrived at Le Bourget airport in 1980 he asked the famous question: "France, eldest daughter of the Church and teacher of peoples, are you being faithful to the promises of your baptism?" The twentieth century was not good for Catholicism in France, any more than in the rest of Europe. A new Pentecost was indeed needed.

Marthe wrote before World War II: "France is going to descend to the depths of the abyss, to the point where no human solution to the problems can be seen. She will be alone, abandoned by all other nations. But she will not remain in this extremity for long. She will not be saved by arms or by any human genius, because no human power will be strong enough. France will be saved, for God will intervene through the Blessed Virgin. It is she who will save France, and the world. The Good Lord will intervene through the Blessed Virgin and the Holy Spirit. There will be a new Pentecost. This new coming of the Holy Spirit will be seen particularly in France, and will indeed realise her mission as eldest daughter of the Church."

Marthe seemed to foresee the appearances of Our Lady at Ile-Bouchard in 1947, the Second Vatican Council, and the spread of the Foyers of Charity throughout the world.

4

The Foundation
of the Foyers

All through the summer of 1936 parishioners began to make preparations in the chateau-turned-school for the first retreat to be preached by Abbé Finet. It was at the end of July that he was present for the first time at her weekly Passion. That same month the socialist *Front Populaire* took control of the government, as Hitler rose to power in Germany, and as the Olympic Games were held in Berlin, revealing the frightening extent of Nazi influence. At the school, dormitories were divided into cubicles by curtains suspended on wires, and washing facilities were rudimentary by today's standards. A chapel was created in the Orangery, using kneelers borrowed from the parish church, and the conferences would be given there.

By 7 September all was ready, and thirty-three mostly middle-aged women, recruited by word of mouth, made their way to Châteauneuf. Among them were two highly qualified teachers from Lyon in their twenties, both known to Georges Finet, Marie-Ange Dumas and Hélène Fagot. The latter wrote a perceptive account of this retreat later on. She was quite reluctant to attend, since another retreat would have been more convenient, but was persuaded by Abbé Finet. On arrival at the chateau she suffered a further shock when she found that nearly everyone else was middle-aged; then she was told that behind it all was a paraplegic mystic ... all rather off-putting! However, on the third day Fr Finet took her and Marie-Ange up to La Plaine, and they met Marthe separately. Both were entirely won over by her. "It was a miracle, for I was really quite ill-disposed."

On the final night, our spiritual enemy showed his displeasure by disturbing the participants with a series of bangs and crashes. Piles of crockery were heard to fall in the kitchen. The sound of a car was heard driving through the dormitory; Hélène turned to Marie-Ange and asked her if she had heard the car. She replied: "In the time of the Curé d'Ars the devil was said to be heard arriving in a horse-drawn carriage ... he must have modernised his transport!" Next day they went up the hill to bid goodbye to Marthe. Hélène and Marie-Ange were then driven to the station by Fr Finet. When he returned to Marthe she confided in him that she was sure the two young teachers would return to take over the school.

The First Community is formed ...

The retreat set the pattern for all future Foyer retreats. Fr Finet gave a series of daily conferences, all containing much solid instruction. There was a night set aside for adoration in the chapel, retreatants watching in turn before the Blessed Sacrament, and the retreat concluded with the consecration to Jesus through Mary, using the formula of St Louis Grignion de Montfort. Hélène admitted later that Marian devotion had not previously been her forte, and that it was through Marthe that she discovered the wonderful maternal side of Mary, balancing the paternal role of the Father in heaven.

It was on the evening of Our Lady's birthday on the 8th that Abbés Faure and Finet brought Holy Communion to Marthe and Georges Finet heard himself addressed for the first time as "Père". It was also the anniversary of his baptism, and he received from Marthe the paternity that he was to share with the Fathers of the Foyers worldwide. From that day Père Finet replaced Abbé Faure.

A few days later, the two young teachers approached Fr Finet independently and offered their services to the school at Châteauneuf. They moved to the chateau on 30 September, and took over the organisation of the twenty-four pupils—the first Foyer community was in existence. In the evenings they would go up to La Plaine and talk with Marthe about the children, the meals, their problems and their lives. Fr Finet would come from Lyon for half the week.

They planned the second retreat for the week between Christmas and the New Year. This too became traditional in many of the Foyers. The retreatants would arrive on Boxing Day and leave on New Year's Day, having spent the final night adoring the Blessed Sacrament. Once again there was a diabolical demonstration, with Fr Finet and one other person being ejected from their beds in the early morning. The local paper reported a mild earthquake, and Marthe said to Fr Finet: "The devil wanted to destroy the Foyer!" From then on the holiday periods were used for retreats, with a majority during "les grandes vacances" in July and August.

Building a New Foyer at Châteauneuf

By 1938, Fr Finet had come to the conclusion that school and Foyer must be separated. This meant building a Foyer alongside the chateau. By this time he was giving retreats to men as well as women; mixed retreats would follow in due course. Thus in May 1939, a year before the German army was to overwhelm Holland, Belgium and France, the foundations of the new building were laid. By the autumn of 1940, France was occupied, the French army had collapsed, and Marshal Pétain, celebrated veteran of the previous war, had negotiated a settlement with the Germans. The so-called "Vichy Regime" administering an unoccupied area of central and southern France, was about to begin; and yet, despite the shortages, the Foyer walls rose. Had not Jesus said to Marthe some years before that they should build despite "the difficulties of the hour"? And with the building came vocations to join the community. Of course Marthe never once saw the Foyer. But she took a close interest in every detail reported to her, and through her constant contact with Fr Finet, and frequent encounters with the members, she may be regarded as the inspirer of the first Foyer. When one sees the Foyer today for the first time, one is amazed at the scale conceived in 1939 by Fr Finet and Marthe.

Defining a Foyer

What exactly was this first Foyer, on which more than seventy have been modelled all over the world? It was neither a convent nor a monastery. Its members were not "religious" in the technical sense, and did not take vows. "A Foyer is a community of baptised Christians, both men and women, who, following the example of the first Christians, (cf. Acts 1), pool their material, intellectual and spiritual goods. They are linked by the love of Jesus and his Mother, as members of the Body of Christ."

Marthe used to say that the Father of the Foyer, the priest, "is the realisation of the Paternity of God." His role is to form, to teach, to guide and to advise, and to welcome guests. With Out Lady as Mother, the whole community is to radiate light, charity and love. The personal love of God, of which St John speaks, is at the root of the life of every Foyer member. In the course of time, Foyers were to be founded in the most diverse ethnic and cultural parts of the world. Jesus had already instructed Marthe as to their nature.

As the Canonical Structures of the Foyers state: "Each Foyer will have its own particular character in order to re-Christianise a variety of peoples. They will act in collaboration with the Centre Foyer (Châteauneuf) to maintain unity with the Church. Each family will not enclose itself behind narrow frontiers, but will go beyond them. Those who come to the foyers, alone or in groups, from whatever nation, are to be received in the same way; for with whatever language or costume they come, they are called to the same unity. In this way their variety will serve to enrich the whole human race, just as a variety of gifts enrich any country or family."

At the time of writing, there are more than seventy Foyers spread over five continents: the mustard-seed has become a huge tree.

Marthe and her Family

A brief examination of Marthe's relationships with the several members of her family is necessary at this point. We have seen how her illness produced certain strains, especially with her father and brother. By the time Fr Finet came on the scene, in 1936, her father had matured a good deal spiritually. As he moved toward his death in June of that year, his faith became considerably more real.

In a letter written to a friend the following month this is what Marthe said:

"The very day the postman brought me your last letter, the soul of my beloved Daddy was taken by Our Lord into Heaven. At the same time my dear Mummy was quite ill, suffering from her liver. So you see why I couldn't write at once. I shall not attempt to describe the moral tortures that I have endured for these last few weeks, seeing both my parents so ill, without being able to give them any physical support. But one great joy has softened my grief, namely that my dearest Daddy really died like a saint, to my great happiness. He spent his final days and nights in prayer, with his hands clasped over his poor chest; towards the end all he could do was to repeat 'Lord, have pity on us.' His last kiss was given to Jesus crucified. May the Lord be ever thanked and glorified for this grace. Oh yes! I hope that our great God of Love will have greeted him, whom he loved so much, and who the week before he died received the last sacraments, for which he had asked."

The Illness and Death of Marthe's Mother

We have a lot more detail concerning the final years of Mme Robin's life. Hélène Fagot recalls: "In 1937 Mme Robin took to her bed and the doctor was called. He probed her stomach, and remarked: 'C'est grave!' On his way to his car he said to me: 'She's not long for this world.' When I returned to their room, (Marthe shared it with her mother), Marthe said: 'On your knees! We are going to start a novena to Our Lady of Lourdes. If mum recovers, she will go to Lourdes.'

"Three or four days later the doctor came back, and I can still see him with his hand on Mme Robin's stomach. 'There's nothing there any more', he said. So Marthe said 'Let's say a prayer of thanks to Our Lady of Lourdes!' A few months later, in 1938, I took Mme Robin to Lourdes by train, rather against her will. We stayed from Monday to Thursday. Lourdes was very crowded, and we had some difficulty in finding a hotel. On the Tuesday we visited the Grotto, and Mme Robin went to confession. We got back to Châteauneuf on Thursday evening, just as Marthe was starting her Passion."

Two years passed. In the autumn of 1940, Mme Robin again fell seriously ill, and was taken to hospital in Lyon, where Dr Ricard, Fr Finet's brother-in-law, operated on her. Hélène was with her, and kept in touch with Marie-Ange at the school by telephone. On Friday 22nd November, Fr Faure arrived to visit the dying patient, with the message: "Marthe says we are to bring her mother home at once." The doctor objected that she might die on the way, but in the end gave permission for her to travel in an ambulance. Hélène and Mère Lautru went too. As they travelled, Marthe was deep into her Passion. They arrived at 5:30 p.m., and Marthe was unconscious. Mme Robin was placed in the bed beside her, and Fr Finet arrived to give her the last sacraments. Shortly afterwards she died. At that moment Marthe began to speak to her mother's soul, which she did for ten minutes, finishing with: "Enter now your eternal dwelling place."

When she emerged from her ecstasy, she confided to Fr Finet: "The Lord asked me to do mother's purgatory. I shall therefore have to suffer more greatly for the next nine months." And indeed both Marthe and Fr Finet went through a very rough period, to the extent that she temporarily lost confidence in her vocation and in the Father, whom she addressed as "Monsieur Finet". He was very distressed and also quite ill. Hélène's comment was: "It was a deep mystery ... I can say no more."

Family Sadness and Joy

A great source of sadness ten years later was the suicide of her brother Henri. After Mme Robin's death the farm had passed to Henri as the only son, but soon members of the Foyer came to live in the house to look after Marthe. Fr Finet got his brother-in-law Dr Ricard to make Henri an offer for the farm he couldn't refuse, and so the Foyer became the legal owner of La Plaine, but Henri continued to live there and run the farm. He was a shy man with a nervous disposition, and often felt a stranger in his own place, particularly when Fr Finet brought more and more visitors to see his bed-ridden sister. It was not a happy situation, and on 8 August 1951 Henri took his shotgun and ended his life. At that time the Church still showed little tolerance to suicides. St Faustina and her teaching on Divine Mercy had not yet impinged on the Church. Marthe loved her brother, (and Godfather), and was deeply upset. But she became convinced that his soul was safe.

There has been speculation as to whether she herself ever contemplated suicide. Like St Thérèse of Lisieux she recommended that strong drugs never be left within reach of a seriously ill person. At all events she always showed great sympathy towards those of her visitors who had lost friends or relatives through suicide.

It was in July 1940 that her sight deteriorated, and with Fr Finet's permission she offered her sight for peace and a conclusion of the war. Thereafter she lived in a room from which light was excluded by shutters and curtains, so that visitors had first to become acclimatised to the semi-darkness. Indeed any sudden light caused Marthe considerable pain, something the bishop who succeeded Mgr Pic failed to comprehend. But even he, having been suspicious of Marthe to start with, eventually accepted her as an extraordinary person.

With her three sisters, all of whom married, Marthe got on famously, and in due course came to love their families. At the end of Raymond Peyret's most recent book (*L'Offrande d'Une Vie*) there is an appendix entitled "Témoignage de la Famille" in which the children and grand-children of Célina, Gabrielle and Alice thank Père Peyret charmingly, for showing them the true face of Marthe as they remember her. They bear witness to her mystical life, accompanied by visions of Mary and also by diabolical attacks, and to the fact that she was totally paralysed and blind, never ate or drank, and bore on her body the marks of Christ's stigmata. "Goodbye and thank you, dearest Aunt Marthe!" She took pleasure in visits from her extended family, and wanted to know all that was going on in the village, just as she wanted to be kept in touch with her beloved Foyer.

The Spread of the Foyers

After World War II, there was much need for reconstruction. Large parts of Europe had been devastated by this terrible war, and both society and its buildings needed restoration. In a real sense the world of before the two world wars had gone for ever, and even the leaders of the Church realised that they would have to rebuild on a different model. Hence the call by Pope John XXIII to summon an Ecumenical Council in 1962, a Council which was to complete the work begun, but interrupted, by the First Vatican Council of 1870. Many new ideas sprang from Vatican II, as it became known, not all of them in keeping with the timeless doctrine of the Church;

but one which was evident and had to be accepted was the increasing role that the laity were to play. This had been foreseen by Marthe in her mystic revelations, and in the post-conciliar Church all kinds of lay initiatives emerged. When John Paul II called a meeting of the new ecclesial movements, mostly involving lay people, in 1998, no fewer than two hundred were represented.

In 1948, twelve years after its humble beginnings in 1936, Mgr Pic of Valence officially inaugurated and blessed the Foyer at Châteauneuf. Fr Finet, who was about to celebrate the 25th anniversary of his ordination, was made a Canon of Valence. By now the first Foyer was well-known and accepted by the Church. The time had come to expand. Three foundations were made before 1949, two in France and one in Belgium. During the 1950's another nine came into being, and seventeen more in the 1960's. No fewer than thirty were started in the 1970's; but not all prospered.

Africa and Beyond ...

The first Foyer to be established in Africa was at the request of the Archbishop of Dakar at Cap les Biches in Senegal. The first in Latin America was started by a young Colombian lady called Laetitia van Hissenhoven; it took her several years. Marthe said to her in 1963: "The Foyer in Colombia will be like a lighthouse illuminating South America." There are now three in Colombia. A foundation was made in Togo in the 60's, and today there are no fewer than twenty-four in Africa alone. They have tended to start, naturally enough, in French speaking parts, and today African bishops are eagerly asking for Foyers. In Asia the first was at Saigon in Vietnam in 1968; today there are ten, including two in India which I have visited. In Europe they are still the most numerous, twenty-five all told, of which half are in France. It has to be noted that the Anglophone area of the world has been hardly penetrated so far. But this will come.

The five day silent retreat remains the principal work of the Foyers, but much variety has been added, such as shorter retreats for young people, and weekends for married couples. A number of the Foyers run schools, notably Châteauneuf, and Courset near Boulogne, and one or two can accommodate up to three hundred retreatants, while new building is going on all the time. The new chapel at Châteauneuf, inaugurated in 1979, is on a truly grand scale; every detail was approved by Marthe herself. Père Michon, the present senior Foyer priest, spends part of each year visiting overseas Foyers, and is often present when new members make their commitment after a three year postulancy. Thus we may see that the vocation of the Foyers is two-fold, missionary and formative. Marthe would dearly have loved to have been able to travel overseas as a missionary, and was conscious that St Thérèse had asked her to carry on her work. She was quite certain that God wished the Foyers to go to every corner of the planet, and having arrived there, to train local lay people to be better Christians.

5

Marthe and Her Visitors

Since Marthe's death her room has become like a shrine, with some forty thousand persons a year coming to visit it. And a record has been kept of all those who met Marthe at La Plaine during her lifetime, and more than a hundred thousand are on it. Allowing for those who came more than once, and also for those whose names were not recorded, the figure is truly astonishing. This happened over a period of half a century. How was this organised?

Marthe was virtually out of action from Friday to Sunday, experiencing her Passions. During the remaining four days a great deal had to be fitted in. For a start there was her voluminous correspondence that had to be dealt with. This of course was entirely the work of her various secretaries. Marthe had an astonishing memory both for the details of her correspondents and for those of her visitors. At one time too, particularly in the early years, parcels were made up in her room and dispatched to prisons, charities, or overseas Foyers. "La Corbeille de Marthe" was a feature in the Centre-Foyer, into which retreatants were invited to place bars of chocolate, packets of cigarettes, rosaries, bibles and holy cards, etc., to be sent to needy people. Nearly all those who came on retreat to Châteauneuf had the opportunity to meet Marthe during the week. A list would be put up, and each one would book a time. Sometimes a queue formed entailing a long delay. They waited in the kitchen and in theory were allowed ten minutes each; but often Marthe overran her time. On arrival in the obscurity of her room, built onto the far side of the farmhouse by Fr Finet when the Foyer took it over, one would give one's name and home town and wait for her to initiate the conversation.

Many are the witnesses who have left a record of their meeting with her. Marthe's voice was clear and youthful; she came quickly to the point with a few pertinent questions, and in nearly every case made helpful comments and suggestions. Her aim seems to have been to lead her visitors to work out a solution to their problems with the help of the Holy Spirit. She did not regard herself, and disliked being regarded, as a kind of oracle or problem solver. She was a remarkable listener. Some of her regular visitors, like Jean Guitton and Marcel Clément, wrote whole books about her, as we will see in due course. Her visitors came from every social, political, and ecclesiastical background.

Cardinal Daniélou wrote; "The most extraordinary person of the century was neither John XXIII nor General de Gaulle, but Marthe Robin." She always concluded her brief interview with a prayer. Her remarkable ten minutes with the successful businessman Yves de Boisredon led to his becoming a priest, and this is his account of what happened.

Yves de Boisredon meets Marthe

"I was born into a believing family. My parents told me that they prayed for me even before I was born; and we always prayed *en famille* morning and evening, and at meals. At about the age of 16 or 17 I was seized by a crazy dream. I was going to make lots of money, so that by the age of 40 I would be rich enough to do whatever I liked with my life. My studies at school had been no more than mediocre, but I threw myself into minor business activities which began to reap rewards. A few years later I was offered a job in a wine exporting business with the prospect that if I was successful I might become the boss. And that is what happened.

"Thus I began to lead the life of a business man travelling around the world for eight months of the year, and reaping whatever advantage I could. In material terms I had everything I had dreamt of . . . I hunted, piloted aeroplanes, and so on; and mothers of eligible daughters held me in high marital esteem.

"But my personal life was becoming seriously downgraded. I was totally indifferent to everything regarding the Faith. I drank more than was good for me. I was smoking at least fifty cigarettes a day. A doctor friend told me one day that if I carried on that way I should risk damaging my brain. This scared me to the extent that I agreed to go away for a complete rest after the end of a planned business trip.

"On my return the doctor rang me up. 'Yves, you remember your promise? Well, I've found just the place.' I waited for a description of some plush four star hotel with swimming-pool, golf course, etc. 'It's called Châteauneuf-de-Galaure, it's a Foyer of Charity, a place where people make retreats.' 'But I've no wish to make a retreat!' 'I know; but do go just the same. The whole thing is in silence, and you don't have to attend the talks if you don't want to; the food is good and the place is comfortable. It's really the ideal place for a rest cure!'

"So I found myself booked for a retreat! That was in July 1980, I arrived one Monday evening and settled into my room with the intention of sleeping as much as possible. However, next morning I awoke feeling fresh at seven o'clock, and with no desire to go back to sleep. So I got up and decided to attend the first conference after breakfast.

"It was Père Finet who was giving the talks. I was quickly struck by the fact that it was perfectly clear that he was a priest. What was more he said things with intelligence and humour which rang true. Lunchtime came. While we were at table another priest took the mike and began to talk about a person called Marthe Robin who was marked with the

Stigmata of Our Lord's Passion, and who every week relived this experience. This puzzled me. But I went to the next conference in the course of which Père Finet warned us against the temptation to pack up and leave. Cut to the quick, I decided I must remain, come what may.

"We were told we might put our names down on a list to visit Marthe, with the proviso that, being a large number, we might not all be able to meet her. I put my name down partly out of curiosity, reckoning that since I was never lucky at gambling I would probably not be one to see her.

"The retreat went on. On Wednesday I went to confession, a reflex from my school retreats. I found Père Finet and went to him. I have the impression that this lasted only about three minutes and I have no precise recollection of it. But I do remember seeing Rembrandt's 'The Prodigal Son' some time later, and thinking that this picture of the tenderness of the Father for his child was exactly what I had experienced during this confession.

"Thursday came, which was the last possible day to see Marthe; and there was my name on the list. Rather anxiously I arrived at 'La Plaine', not knowing too well what I was going to say to her. I waited in the kitchen. When my turn came I went into her darkened room and sat on the little chair beside her couch.

"Bonjour!"

"Bonjour . . . my name is Yves de Boisredon. I'm 33 and I export wine."

"Ah yes . . . are you enjoying the retreat?"

"Yes. I like Père Finet a lot."

"Do you know the Foyers of Charity?"

"I told her how I had gone one year to the Port-au-Prince Foyer for the Midnight Mass. Then she said: 'You know at your age you should be contemplating marriage or the priesthood or consecrated celibacy.'

"I can hear myself replying: 'Can one be thinking of the priesthood at the age of 33?' " Marthe then asked me what studies I had done, and whether I had ever learnt Latin or Greek. Then she said: 'You know, you can't wait ten years or you will be driving alongside your own road. Now would you like to pray with me?'

"I knelt beside her bed and heard her begin the Hail Mary in a voice of extraordinary tenderness. At that moment tears came gushing from my eyes. I could not believe one could cry like that, yet at the same time I felt no embarrassment. At the end of the prayer I murmured a goodbye. She answered with 'Goodbye and thank you.'

"I went out into the courtyard and there had an experience which is difficult to describe, extremely sweet and powerful. The best way to speak of it is to evoke the episode of the rich young man in the Gospel: 'Jesus looked at him and loved him.' At that precise moment the world changed for me. I put my head in my hands and said to myself: 'Yves, you're a priest!' Tears poured forth more abundantly, but I felt an extraordinary peace and joy. This was accompanied by total certainty and security: nothing and no one would be able to remove that peace from me.

"Having said this, however, my brain started to react violently. 'But you're going crazy . . . a rascal like you has never turned into a priest!'

"I decided I must see Père Finet as soon as possible. There was a queue of thirty people waiting at his door! Next day the same thing. I went on following the retreat; each time I saw a priest or heard the priesthood mentioned tears welled into my eyes. On Friday there was a whole conference on the subject, and I got through most of my Kleenex. Finally at midday on the Sunday I managed to speak to him. He gave me an appointment for the afternoon. I told him what had happened. 'Well, it is quite simple', he said, 'you are going to become a priest. You will do the necessary studies, and all will go well. And now I will give you my blessing.'

"We fell into each other's arms and I began to cry, and he blessed me.

"Fifteen months later I entered the seminary. There I met members of the Emmanuel Community, to which I soon felt called. Community life was a great support in my journey towards ordination. This took place in June 1987 in the diocese of Paris. I was then 40."

Marthe did not pretend to be able to solve all her visitor's problems. Indeed, in the case of priests and religious, she usually recommended them to consult their own superiors. To quote just one story; a nun came and poured out her problems and dissatisfactions; Marthe listened in silence and then simply said: "Glory be to the Father and to the Son and to the Holy Spirit."

But the fact remains that many thousands came away from her refreshed and reinvigorated: it was a remarkable apostolate. To a priest who thanked her for having underlined the importance of the sign of the cross she said: "The cross is embedded in my body, my soul, and my heart." There is a lot more that could be written in this context, as Père Peyrous says in his recent book: "A whole book could be written on the advice and good sense she offered to countless people." He also tells us that from the '70s she became increasingly concerned about the question of abortion. "People get indignant over the killing in war, but do nothing to stop this massacre of the innocents. Can this be normal? Surely these babies suffer?"

Marthe and the Priesthood

Marthe had an especially high regard for the priesthood, and we shall now look at her many relationships with priests. Even in childhood she always saw them as special people. First in her life was the Abbé Cluze who prepared her for her first Holy Communion at the age of ten. Because she and the schoolteacher's son had been ill a few weeks earlier, he gave them a special preparation and their First Holy Communion on 15 August 1912, about which she wrote years later: "I think Our Lord took possession of me at that moment." Then there was Abbé Faure, who, despite his awkwardness, did serve her spiritually over many years. Abbés Perrier and Betton should be mentioned, and the Capuchin Père Bernard. Finally, of course, came Père Finet, who was her spiritual father for forty-five years.

On 22 January 1930, she wrote a remarkable piece regretting, in a way, that she had never had the good fortune to study theology as priests do. "But still, does not prayer and divine contemplation exceed by far in knowledge, love and power the most profound studies? Experience is deeper, more enlightening and more fruitful than science. For me all my theology and my science is love, the union of my soul with God through Jesus Christ with the Blessed Virgin! Nothing more, nothing less."

Many priests came to consult her over the years, after 1936, and she came to realise that not a few were less than faithful to the vows of their calling, which always upset her considerably. Often she would mention this during her passions. She knew of their difficulties and temptations, and many had asked her to uphold them in her prayer. Many have testified to the good influence she had on them: after meeting her, they felt closer to the supernatural, and spiritually revived.

Here is just one such testimony: "If I remain a priest today, I owe it largely to the prayer and offering of Marthe. I am of the generation of May 1968 when, influenced by the seminaries of the time, we questioned everything. Many of our elders were giving up their ministry, as indeed did my own spiritual father. The rumour was circulating that Paul VI would soon allow priests to marry. This 'wind of madness' nourished the tempest in my heart. It was thus that I came to Châteauneuf in 1970 and was taken to meet Marthe in her darkened room. What I chiefly recall were the silences, and the few soft sentences spoken by Marthe. It was two months later, on Holy Thursday, that I suddenly understood the nature of the priesthood to which I was called. Peace and joy overwhelmed my heart and have never left me. The sacrifice of Marthe had overcome all the powers of darkness." A certain Canon Bérardier, who visited her in 1942, wrote: "Speaking about the priesthood, I was amazed at the way this country girl used language that might have come from the superior of a seminary."

Marthe's Holy Communions

All those who had the privilege of giving Holy Communion to Marthe, which she received once a week on Wednesdays, testify to the fact that as the host approached her lips it seemed to escape from their hands and disappear into her mouth without her appearing to swallow. After all, she ate no ordinary food for fifty years. And immediately afterwards she would be in ecstasy. Raymond Peyret wrote: "It was priests who taught Marthe the rudiments of the Faith and initiated her into prayer and the spiritual life. But she gave back in full to the sacerdotal body what she received from it. Her experience was more instructive for priests than many lectures given in the seminary. Those who met Marthe will never forget her essential recommendation—to be holy, to go out to others, and never to abandon prayer, however busy their work."

He finishes his chapter on the priesthood with extended quotations from the diary of a local priest, the Curé of Saint-Vallier, Père Vignon. Written in March 1943, at the height (or depth) of the occupation of France, he tells in some detail of a visit he made to see Marthe. She was going through a bad patch, and was both pessimistic and optimistic about the sufferings of the time. What upset her most were the reports of the deportation to Germany of young Frenchmen, some of whom had been to see her and had wept bitterly. As always, recourse to prayer was her only answer ... il faut prier. She contrasted Communism, which so many French people now favoured, with "Hitlerism," (as she called it), concluding that the former was less terrible. How to stir up the half-hearted Christians, whose practise was largely external, that was the problem. Fr Vignon stayed in the presbytery and witnessed the start of a Passion on Thursday evening. It was clear that Marthe was suffering tremendously. At 11 p.m. Fr Finet locked her door and the two priests went on their way. Next day Vignon returned to La Plaine after his Mass. Marthe was still groaning, and her face was covered with blood issuing from her eyes and forehead. It was a heart-rending scene. At 2 p.m. he returned to his parish on the bus.

This is the Prayer for Priests composed by Marthe:

"Take your priests, O my God, fully and entirely, to accomplish or at least to help to accomplish all that You wish of them. Lead them in everything. Be their strength, O my God. May all their actions, whether important or unimportant, come to them from You, depend on You, and be addressed to You. May they be all for You, O my God, to glorify You, to love you and to make you loved. My God, set our hearts on fire with your Love; fill us with your Divine Joy. O Father, spread throughout the world and over souls your supreme Mercy and your divine Pardon. My God, show your love to France and to the whole world; re-establish peace and order on earth. Lead all people to unity, O my God, and unite their spirits and hearts in You."

6

The Foyer Schools and the Sick

There is a profound connection between the Foyers and their schools; these were not haphazard accretions. The first school and the first Foyer at Châteauneuf are intimately linked; they were foreseen together by Marthe and form a single whole. Marthe used to say humorously that the school was a branch of the Foyer though it had started first! She herself maintained a close contact with pupils, parents and teachers throughout her life. She was convinced that parents and school must collaborate closely; they must not think that sending their children to Châteauneuf abdicated their responsibility to pass on the Faith to their offspring. In October 1976 she said to some new parents: "If you have chosen this school, it is not to make things easier for you. You have to accept your responsibilities. Either you must become fully involved, or else you must send them elsewhere!" And again: "The family must become involved with us, or else we can do nothing. We must be in harmony with each other. Prayer is necessary for unity."

Thus friendship and collaboration was encouraged between parents and teachers, and official meetings to discuss both scholarship and spirituality were arranged. Marthe summed up the role of the educator as follows: "In each child we must see the Lord who inhabits that soul, look at it with the eyes of Jesus and with the eyes of the Holy Virgin."

Marthe often emphasised the importance of family prayers. "It is so vital that parents pray with their children around them." "The mission of the mother is to form the soul of her child ... unity of heart and soul is essential. Children always feel the lack of unity." But her approach was always that of invitation, never of reproach. She loved to receive groups of pupils with their teachers into her room. On one occasion they recalled this advice given before the holiday break: "Mass is not an obligation ... it is a necessity! Are you going to leave Jesus for the holidays? So, talk with your parents, pray every morning and evening, offer your day to God. Say some rosary wherever you may be, and go to confession regularly. Be a witness to Jesus during the holidays."

In 1973, someone asked her what her mission was, and Fr Finet recorded her significant reply: "It is to offer myself. My life is a continual Mass. I never think of my bed as only a bed, but rather as an altar, on the cross." One pupil who went through the girls school and eventually became a teacher recalls how frightened she was to meet Marthe as a younger girl, but how inspired she felt when meeting her alone as a leaver. She felt refreshed and transported with joy. Clearly Marthe had an excellent relationship with the pupils, even in old age. She was interested in each one, and loved them all. Many teachers, too, testify to the way Marthe encouraged them to get onto the level of their charges, just as members of the Foyer were encouraged to support the retreatants.

She was not keen on the growing popularity of mixed education. This was no panacea for emotional problems. Boys and girls needed a different formation. In 1949 she met a chaplain from a Parisian school and said to him: "It's a good thing to shake them up occasionally. We all need shaking up! You too!" "Be demanding of them" was another of her sayings. Although cut off in the solitude of her room, she had an extraordinarily practical sense of what was required in a good school, and she followed the development of the Foyer schools closely.

Marthe and the Sick

The value of sickness and suffering in God's work of redemption, which used to be emphasised in Catholic theology, is quite neglected today, although it has been expressed in great literature, such as the following remark of Cordelia Flyte regarding Sebastian, in *Brideshead Revisited*: "No one is holy without suffering."

It can only be made sensible in terms of love. Marthe said: "Love alone attracts me. I no longer desire suffering, but I possess it. And by means of it I believe I have touched the very shores of heaven! Today I have nothing more to ask of Jesus, except the perfect accomplishment of his adorable will and his infinite love." And, like Jesus, Marthe took upon herself all human suffering. It was a vocation reserved for very few: "Do you want to be like me?"

Marthe's great desire is expressed very well in Psalm 63:

O God, you are my God, earnestly I seek you;
my soul thirsts for you, my body longs for you,
in a dry and weary land where there is no water.
I have seen you in the sanctuary
and beheld your power and your glory.
Because your love is better than life,
my lips will glorify you.
I will praise you as long as I live,
and in your name I will lift up my hands.
My soul will be satisfied as with the richest of foods;
with singing lips my mouth will praise you.
On my bed I remember you; I think of
you through the watches of the night.
Because you are my help, I sing in the shadow of your wings.
My soul clings to you; your right hand upholds me.

We are given plenty of examples in the Gospels of how Jesus cured sick people. And He told his disciples that they would have the same power. Clearly God wishes all people to be whole, physically and mentally. But in our world, deeply affected by the Fall, there are many who are not whole. This scandalises the average non-Christian, and the desire to eliminate illness and handicap lies behind the support for such dangerous issues as abortion and stem-cell research. The Christian solution hinges, as ever, on prayer, and the belief that God can make the un-whole whole. And the Church believes that holy people can exercise this influence by their prayer, which is why it still insists on a major miracle of healing before it will beatify or canonise a saint.

St Gregory the Great in his commentary on the Book of Job wrote: "Those justified in the sight of God (in other words the saints) can be recognised in this way ... weighed down by painful trials, they do not cease from being concerned with others. They are great healers, while at the same time often struck by illness. Wounded themselves, they bring to others the remedies for health." This could apply exactly to Marthe. She once said to Gisèle Signé: "People often ask me to pray for them, and then forget to keep me *au fait* with their progress." She liked to hear of the answers to her prayers. We do know, however, that she obtained many favours, some of which are recorded in *The Cross and the Joy*, Raymond Peyret's first biography. Three striking examples are included in his latest book *L'Offrande d'une Vie*; one concerned a baby girl aged 13 months dying of pneumonia in 1930, who recovered against all the odds; the second concerned a boy of six who, in 1936, recovered from a serious attack of pleurisy; and the third concerned the boy's mother who underwent a serious operation the following year, and who, on recovering, went to thank Marthe in 1938. There must be no shortage of cases being presented by the Postulator of her cause in Rome, although these will involve cures coming after Marthe's death, and brought about through her intercession.

There is a fascinating story told by Marguerite Lautru who had asked Marthe to embroider a dress for one of her little cousins. She never actually saw her using her needles. When she gave the dress to her cousin she said: "Take good care of this dress." And in fact it was kept for years unused in a cupboard. Ten or fifteen years later Marthe herself enquired after the girl who had been given the dress. About the same time the girl returned the dress to Marguerite, and she remarked to Marthe that she had never seen her do the embroidery. She replied: "But it wasn't I who embroidered it!" "So, who did do it?" "It was the Blessed Virgin!" That dress has been used to help many sick persons.

A recent testimony has been given by a retired nurse from Lyon, who was living with her parents near Valence towards the end of Marthe's life. In September 1980, her father was suffering greatly from cancer of the throat, and she called the ambulance to take him to hospital. Meanwhile she and her mother invoked the help of Marthe. Suddenly the father began to recover and the ambulance was sent away. The doctors were amazed.

Marthe and the New Pentecost

As we have seen, one of the intriguing things said by Marthe to Fr Finet, on 10 February 1936, was that God had foretold a new Pentecost of Love that would be preceded by a renewal of the Church. And the laity were to have an important role to play, notably in the Foyers of Light, Charity and Love. The years passed, and no serious evidence of this was apparent. However, when Pius XII, John XXIII, and Paul VI all spoke of a "new springtime in the Church", Fr Finet began to wonder whether the prophecy would be fulfilled. After Vatican II there was a liturgical renewal, though this has proved controversial. It would not be unfair to say, however, that the reformed rite of Paul VI is seen at its best in the Foyers. A great many ecclesial movements have originated in the twentieth century, some of which will be examined further on, since Marthe was known to many of them. Finally there has been a "Charismatic Renewal" within the Catholic Church, and some of the Foyers feature it. Thus, while on the one hand the Church—particularly in the "First World" of Europe and North America—has appeared to be losing ground to secularism and materialism, on the other it has shown genuine signs of a "New Pentecost", and there have been unprecedented assemblies of Christians on a grand scale, particularly associated with the pilgrim journeys of John Paul the Great, and the World Youth Days he initiated.

Marthe, like St Louis de Montfort, laid great stress on the Holy Spirit, and in May 1939 wrote a wonderful eulogy to the Third Person of the Blessed Trinity. Together with prayer and praise, which are hallmarks of the Foyers, Marthe saw in the Charismatic Renewal a means of evangelisation. This was to be the main apostolate of all the Foyers, to deepen the faith of the retreatants during their time of withdrawal, and so ultimately spread the Gospel of Jesus Christ. The restoration of authentic Christian communities, as seen in the Foyers, is shared with Charismatic communities whose life-style may differ in certain respects.

7

Jean Guitton and Marthe

Among the hundred thousand people who had heard about Marthe and took the trouble to meet her in her room at La Plaine, there were a certain number who were quite distinguished and well-known in her generation, whom we should look at more closely. Indeed several of them have written whole books on her. Of these, perhaps the most famous was Jean Guitton, philosopher, prolific writer, and member of the *Académie Française*, whose book *Portrait de Marthe Robin* was published by Grasset in 1985, just four years after her death, and dedicated to Père Finet. He says of Marthe in his preface that "she was without doubt the most unusual, extraordinary, and disconcerting being of our time." He tells us that he was introduced to her by Anatole France's doctor, who was a disciple of Loisy—the modernist cleric who was excommunicated in 1908—and deeply anti-Christian, but he felt that as soon as he got to know Marthe he had a presentiment that one day he would have to write a book about her.

Guitton stresses that his account is firmly based on his own observations and not on the reports of others, and that, while not playing down the paranormal or mystical elements in her life, he takes the prudent line he has always followed in his studies. He reckons he spent a total of forty hours with her over a period of twenty-five years, and he reminds his readers that, like the work of a painter, his "portrait" is a personal interpretation, and that much has been omitted. I cannot summarise the whole book, but I shall try and pick out the main themes.

Right at the beginning, he defines Marthe as a mystic, and a mystic of the first order. A mystic, he says, has immediate contact with reality, that is the Creator, and Marthe in her ecstasies was familiar with every mystical state. He comments on the dropping of the first atomic bombs in 1945—which he considered a watershed date in modern history—and the fact that Marthe lived through that crucial period in a terrible century which witnessed a scientific reductionism of the spiritual by the followers of Marx and Freud. This trend even secured a following among certain Catholics.

The Sceptical Doctor

Guitton first met Marthe in the company of a well-known doctor who was a religious sceptic, and even doubted the very existence of Jesus Christ; his name was Paul-Louis Couchoud. At one point during the war Guitton had been a prisoner of the Germans. On his release in 1945 he visited a cousin who offered to take him to Châteauneuf, but Fr Finet—whom he refers to as a Cerberus—declined to allow him to see Marthe. His friend Dr Couchoud, however, had heard about Marthe and was determined to visit her, so they wrote to Cardinal Gerlier of Lyon and he persuaded Fr Finet to allow them to meet Marthe. Thus began a somewhat improbable friendship, and the reactions and comments of both men are detailed in Guitton's book.

Dr Couchoud told Guitton that he did not find it difficult to believe that Marthe had the stigmata: many Catholics have been similarly marked. What he found more perplexing was the claim that she did not eat or drink or sleep. He believed that these phenomena gave her a special mental strength, and that her brain-power was developed to an unusual degree. He said that the person she reminded him of when he was with her was Pascal, whose seventeenth century "thoughts" still astonish his readers. He noticed that she was very reticent to speak about "le merveilleux" (or the paranormal) even though it surrounded her like wild grass. He saw in her view of the Foyers an imaginative strategy: "Her idea is that in order that love may reign over the earth at the end of the twentieth century, social classes must be brought together and social conflict suppressed. Employers and employees, priests and lay people, men and women, bishops and faithful, all must be brought to live together as in the first Christian communities. ... This will happen in the retreats which the Foyers will organise all over the world; and from these first sparks will grow a veritable furnace. ...That is Marthe's principal idea."

Couchoud went on to describe how she needed an active collaborator to fulfil this mission, and how Fr Finet had come to her from Lyon to fill this role. He likened their meeting to Joan of Arc encountering the Dauphin. He went on to describe how Fr Finet began to build on a grand scale without the necessary money, and how donations for this nevertheless poured in; and he quoted Jesus' saying: "Seek ye first the kingdom of God, and all these things shall be added unto you." (Mt 6:33)

All this came from a non-practising and non-believing Frenchman! He once said to Marthe: "You know I do not have the faith." To which she replied: "I will carry you in my prayer. But God is ready to open the door to you. And you would not be looking for Him if He had not already found you." Thus she adapted the famous saying of Pascal. And in conversation she explained how it is God who always acts first, which she illustrated with the conversion of St Paul. He also noted that whereas Marthe was very advanced in the mystical life, her devotional practice was fairly simple, and he quoted her as saying "God and Christ are all I need ... and Our Lady's tenderness, because she loves and helps us."

His conclusion was: "I have seen one of the strangest people on the planet. After her death the Holy Office will deal with her. What I fear is that she will perform miracles. One day I said to her: 'Marthe you are nothing other than a brain', to which she replied: 'Don't you think I am also a heart?' " Finally he mentions the diabolical attacks on Marthe, similar to those against St John Vianney. He cannot explain them, but quotes Hamlet's famous saying: "There are more things in heaven and earth, Horatio, than are dreamt of in our philosophy." On taking his leave of Marthe she suggested they embrace, and as he kissed her forehead he saw a drop of blood.

Supernatural Aspects

In his own appraisal of Marthe, Guitton makes no attempt to play down the supernatural elements in her story. On the contrary, he sees destiny, (i.e. the hand of God), in many of the unusual aspects of it. For example, he cites the drama of 13 November 1930, when Fr Finet was miraculously saved from being buried, along with twenty-three others, in the earthquake that hit Lyon, just when Marthe was praying for the priest who was to join her six years later. He emphasises how her life became transformed and fulfilled after their meeting in February 1936. It was an astonishing combination—on the one hand the man of action, and on the other the bed-ridden stigmatic. Guitton sees Grignion de Montfort and Our Lady behind this partnership. He also mentions a more modern saint, Maximilian Kolbe, who, when he wrote his book, had not yet been canonised.

Their great strength, like that of all religious reformers, was to simplify complex issues and make them accessible to ordinary people. Guitton gives a wonderful account of the first meeting between Marthe and Fr Finet—a "moment of destiny" he calls it. She spoke with such assurance and authority that Fr Finet was overwhelmed. Marthe's plan was quite simple; it was nothing less than to evangelise the modern world through five day retreats in silence, in which lay people would be formed by hearing the fundamentals of the Gospel message.

At the same time Guitton traces the growth of the physical handicaps that overtook Marthe from 1918 to 1928, by which time she was bed-ridden, paralysed and unable even to embroider. It was from that time until her death fifty-three years later that her only food was the Blessed Sacrament. He quotes at length the medical report of Drs Dechaume and Ricard (Fr Finet's brother-in-law) who examined Marthe in 1942. Guitton recalls his dozen visits, and conjures up the strong impression left to him of the wait around the stove in the kitchen before penetrating into her darkened room. He remarks how she lived in more or less total darkness for all those years while talking about Foyers of Light. Going into her catacomb, he says, one was blinded by the darkness.

And so Marthe was more or less just a voice; it was that which revealed her. He gives a wonderful description of the richness and variety of that voice; many have given their impressions of her voice, and nearly all emphasise its youthfulness. The other thing he noted in particular was her remarkable grasp of language. He remarks on the astonishing way in which she adapted her conversation to suit the needs of an incredible variety of visitors with a whole range of problems. He quotes his wife who came several times with him as saying: "Elsewhere there are only problems ... with Marthe there are only solutions." She had the gift of going straight to the heart of a problem. In a delightful scriptural analogy, Guitton says that Marthe was as if on Jacob's ladder, able to climb up and down between earth and heaven. "When talking with her in her darkened room, one felt at unity with oneself, with all the others who had been to see her, and with God." Another strange feature was that she seemed to be at home when talking about various parts of the world, as if she had travelled widely.

Conversations with Marthe

In one chapter, Guitton reproduces conversations with Marthe as he recalls them. Like Belloc in his *Path to Rome* he suddenly interrupts his account with conversation, heading the paragraphs "Moi" and "Elle". He gives examples of her sense of humour: "The devil is always active, ready to create confusion. In the old days monks heard the confessions of nuns ... now I am told some want to marry them!" Guitton questions her about her mystical life, and receives some fascinating answers. She insists that the images that she is given, for example during her Passions, are unimportant, and that she has progressed beyond them to the essence of things. At one point she tells Guitton that what he calls "the mystical life" is as much within him as in her. "It consists of trying to be one with Jesus." She speaks too about Guitton's books which she finds difficult at times, and the difference between the Word and eloquence.

He tries to question her about the future, but she will not be drawn into prophecy. However, occasionally she lets slip some thought about how the world is developing; she fears the spread of atomic weapons. Her answer is to offer herself in suffering for the sins of mankind. It was the same reaction that the children at Fatima had. She speaks of the devil, whom she seems to know quite well; how beautiful he appears to be and how clever he is. But it is always possible to overcome him, especially by invoking the Blessed Virgin. Marthe is also familiar with the angels. When asked who her favourite saints are, she replies: "Joan of Arc, because she loved Jesus and the Church, and Thérèse of the Child Jesus, because I saw her in visions." Guitton was a personal friend of Paul VI, and Marthe questions him closely on that post-conciliar pope; she urges him to be firm and not to abdicate (as was rumoured).

She admits to Guitton that at times she longs to die, but that Fr Finet will not give her permission. She foresees that the chief difference in life after death will be the cessation of pain; her chief joy then will be to skip and jump ... but she will not forget those she has loved on earth. When Guitton asked her what she imagined a new Pentecost of Love would be like, she replied: "Oh, nothing extraordinary. I see it coming slowly, little by little; it may even have begun. As for the future, people think I have ideas on the subject. I know only one thing for certain—the future is Jesus." Then she said to him: "I hope you will have the evening meal with us. You will sit at the table where I used to eat with my parents, and I shall listen to the sound of spoons on the plates ..."

Mystical Elements

In a remarkable chapter headed "Les dictées," Guitton selects from the many notebooks filled by Marthe's various scribes. We are left in no doubt at all that she is an exceptional mystic. One day, when she is beatified, some of these writings will be published; meanwhile the quotations selected by Guitton are extremely valuable. In her famous prayer to Our Lady, said each morning in the Foyers, Marthe asks her to "teach us to lift our minds and hearts often to God, and to fix our loving attention on the Trinity". In August 1932, she dictated some quite remarkable thoughts on the nature of the Trinity, and this was four years before she met Fr Finet and founded the first Foyer! Another notable quote was from 1 August 1942, when she gave a description of how she saw the Blessed Virgin. Guitton likens it to that of St Catherine Labouré at the Rue du Bac chapel in 1830.

Guitton explains that in his youth it was not considered good form in academic circles to discuss the mystical elements in religion. There was a sense of reserve on the continent, as in Britain. Even Teresa of Avila and John of the Cross were regarded with reserve. It was his meeting with Henri Bergson at the École Normale that changed his attitude; Bergson was well read in the Christian mystics and indeed regarded Christ as the chief mystic. In this way Guitton, sitting at the feet of

Bergson, who had discovered the mystics late in life, became familiar with this spiritual phenomenon in his formative years. And so he studied the lives of those Christians who, in our own times, featured in Fr John Saward's first book *Perfect Fools*, from St Paul to St Thérèse of Lisieux. Guitton also cites William James's *The Varieties of Religious Experience*, which Lady Soames, daughter of Winston Churchill, introduced him to. James argued that every religion produced its mystics. But Bergson found Christian mystics to be on a different level, and saw in the poor, the pure-hearted, and the persecuted, a profound union with God, equal to those who experienced ecstasy and visions. And in his visits to Marthe, Guitton could see the same thing, someone who had reached beyond ecstasy and visions to the very essence of God. Reduced to the condition of complete humility, such a mystic could share with Jesus what St Paul described in chapter 2 of his Epistle to the Philippians.

Strange Phenomena

Guitton examines some of the stranger phenomena in Marthe's life; for example he recounts how when Marie-Ange Dumas—one of the two original members of the Châteauneuf Foyer—was dying, Marthe came mystically to pray with her, and her voice was overheard by a fellow teacher who came to bid Marie-Ange farewell. Such evidence of bilocation occurs in the stories of many saints, (recently Padre Pio). These things are to a large extent inexplicable—the relation between psychic and physical is a mystery. What do we know, for example, of the relation between matter and memory, the brain and thought? With Marthe, Guitton plumbs the depths of the normal and the paranormal, the natural and the supernatural, more profoundly than any of her other biographers.

In an interesting chapter headed "After Hiroshima", he points out that Marthe was roughly halfway through her life when this extraordinary event in the history of the human race occurred. Few philosophers have grappled with it; even Vatican II ignored it. In general, few "thinkers" have really faced up to the destructive possibilities of nuclear power. In a similar category come the advances in medical science, such as embryonic research and cloning. Indeed, the whole question of the relationship between faith and science is still in its early stages.

Because Marthe lived her long life in such a different way to most people, Guitton is able to reflect on problems of time and space in relation to her. He also reflects on the exceptional length of time that she did not eat or drink. "The case of Marthe lies on the frontier between the improbable and the impossible." Thus the only explanation is to use the term "miraculous". He remarks that in this post-conciliar age it is no longer "theologically correct" to dwell on the word "sacrifice" or to mention "blood". Yet both are bound up intimately in the life of Marthe; he contrasts the appalling violence and bloodshed of two world wars and the effects of the various Communist regimes, with the apparent squeamishness of theologians over the blood of Christ shed in sacrifice to atone for the sins of humankind. Blood is the symbol of life. Not only did Marthe shed blood literally through her stigmata, but every week she offered herself as a kind of holocaust by uniting herself with the Passion of Christ.

Marthe and the Passion

Guitton subtly links Marthe's weekly Communion, (on a Tuesday or Wednesday), with her weekly Passion, and he stresses the extraordinary juxtaposition of the ordinary and the sublime that struck him every time he visited her. "At first sight there was nothing to be seen in that room, where so much went on." She told Guitton that her physical sufferings could not compare with the moral sufferings she also experienced. At times she felt utterly rejected; and as the Second letter to the Corinthians suggests that Christ "became

sin" (5:21) in order to save mankind, so too in a way did
Marthe. She believed that the misfortune of the twentieth
century was the separation between mankind and God, and in
a real sense she represented the whole of humanity in her
suffering.

Guitton notes that the horrors and suffering at Verdun
cannot be reproduced, which is why there is no really fine
book written in French on the First World War, nor can there
be. No other being in that century suffered the Passion of Our
Saviour with such regularity and intensity, and Guitton
quotes Fr Finet as saying: "Jesus told her that she had been
chosen to live the Passion more fully than anyone since the
Blessed Virgin, and that no one subsequently would do so
with such totality."

Guitton questioned Marthe on this at some length. Here is
one question and answer. "Did you have the impression that it
was a phenomenon given once and for all, or that it would be
repeated?" "Oh no! Right from the start I understood that it
would be for always. But, I repeat, it has become ever more
intimate and interior. For several years I have no longer been
on the cross exteriorly. I am, so to speak, the cross. The cross
is in me and I am in the cross, and I have told you that in my
visions, at the beginning, I recognised people who saw Jesus
going up to Calvary. I heard shouts. Now I have moved
beyond that; I would say that this no longer interests me.
What does interest me is the Passion, and Jesus alone. I don't
know how to explain it to you ... these things are so painful
that if God was not sustaining me, I should die. Yet at the
same time it is delightful."

Thoughts about Marthe and her Stigmatisation

Here is a very moving paragraph that Guitton wrote to sum
up his impression of Marthe: "She was as simple as fresh bread
or as milk direct from the cow, like a spring morning or a
fireside conversation. She was like the Way to Emmaus, like
the breaking of bread, like life by the lakeside ... sweet, calm,

familiar, the only sounds being the lapping of water, the noise of wooden shoes, and the laughter of children. Around her was woven the great and the small, the height and the depth, the familiar and the sublime. Her's was a human face at its most strange and at its most commonplace."

If he was never present at one of her Passions, at least he witnessed one of her Communions. Surprisingly, on that occasion there were a dozen girls from the school in her little room at the same time, and she chatted with them. Then the priest arrived in a white surplice. As he brought the Host towards Marthe's mouth, it simply disappeared. The texts that came to Guitton's mind were those sayings of St Paul: "I fill up those things that are wanting of the sufferings of Christ, in my flesh," (Col 1:24) or again: "I live, now not I; but Christ lives in me," (Gal 2:20). In subsequent Masses he could not help imagining Marthe with Christ at the altar.

In the matter of her stigmatisation in October 1930, the descriptions given by Raymond Peyret in the early biographies are drawn from what Guitton tells us Marthe said to him. Strangely the most recent biography by her postulator largely ignores the vital testimony given by Jean Guitton. A great deal of research is still required to throw adequate light on this strange phenomenon, experienced by numerous saints, the best known of whom are St Padre Pio, St Francis of Assisi and St Catherine of Siena. Without doubt Guitton's evidence is of prime importance. In the same chapter he questions Marthe on the fact that the Blessed Sacrament was her only nourishment for so long, and also on her mystical journeys. "When one understands God's love for us," she said to him, "one discovers that eternity will not be long enough for us to thank him." Marthe never read anything on the subject of stigmatisation, nor did the word ever pass her lips. It all relates, of course, to the suffering of our Blessed Lord on the Cross at Calvary, and both are deep mysteries. Efforts to represent this suffering, as in the film by Mel Gibson, are inevitably inadequate and exterior.

Like St John Vianney, and many others, Marthe was very conscious of the opposition of the devil. She usually referred to him simply as "he." Guitton has a short chapter which deals with Satan. As he says, he is neither a psychiatrist nor an exorcist but merely an observer. He would prefer the words at the end of the *Pater Noster* to be translated "but deliver us from the evil one" (*le malin*). Clearly he found that Marthe had an almost daily experience of "le malin", and was well aware of his influence. After all we are told that Lucifer (the light bearer) can disguise himself as an angel of light, and is the father of lies. But he entirely lacks love. In the case of Marthe he was able to attack her body, knocking it around and finally throwing it onto the floor, but he had no power over her soul.

Marthe's Passing and Legacy

And so we come to Guitton's description of Marthe's death on Friday 6 February 1981. She had lived for many years on the threshold of heaven, and had survived until nearly the age of eighty. He makes no mention of the crisis within the Foyer organisation, which Père Peyrous describes in his *Vie de Marthe Robin*, and which undoubtedly had upset her considerably. One aspect of this crisis was that in the late seventies Fr Finet was no longer consulting Marthe as he had previously, and decisions were being taken without her knowledge. Marthe had said to Guitton earlier: "Where shall I go if Fr Finet is no longer here? Would you have room for me in your cottage?" She certainly hoped to die first.

He quotes what Fr Finet told him of Marthe's end. He had not expected her to die, even though she was so old, and unwell after Christmas, or he would not have delayed going to her room until after five o'clock on Friday afternoon. He found her lying on the floor in an evidently disturbed room, and as he and a Foyer member lifted her body back onto her divan he heard her say: "He has killed me." This was not recorded by Père Peyrous, who suggested that she was able to get out of her bed but was too weak to get back into it. They then summoned the doctor and the other Foyer priests, and later the Bishop of Valence, Mgr. Marchand. They dressed her in a white baptismal garment, and throughout the weekend a succession of visitors filed through her room to pay their final respects.

One of the last sayings that Guitton recalls was: "When I leave this world, I shall be more active than I am now ... I intend to take no rest ..." which reminds us of St Thérèse's famous saying: "I shall spend my heaven doing good upon earth." On 10 February, anniversary of her first meeting with Fr Finet, her body was placed in the new church, and two days later the funeral took place, attended by five bishops, over two hundred priests and six thousand of the faithful. Guitton himself was unable to reach Châteauneuf in time, being held up by traffic jams. Her body was laid to rest in the family vault at Saint-Bonnet. "Unless the grain of wheat falling into the ground dies, it remains alone. But if it dies, it brings forth much fruit," said Mgr Marchand in his homily, (cf. Jn 12:24-25).

Marthe in the Context of her Times

In his final chapter Guitton tries to situate Marthe and her life in the broader framework of our times. Writing in 1985, towards the end of his life, he makes it clear that he believes the twentieth century to have been crucial in the history of *Homo sapiens*, and he is inclined to agree with those who see the world hastening towards "the last times". He recalls the crossing of the Channel by his compatriot Bleriot in his youth, and the extraordinary advance in aviation since then. He considers the landing on the moon of Neil Armstrong and his fellow astronauts in the sixties, and the evolution of the computer since the 1940s. Mankind is in an entirely new situation, which he calls "post-historic", for which Hiroshima was the turning point. Since then the human race has been in a position to commit suicide. He says that Marthe was fully conscious of the drama of her times, even though her life was "un voyage immobile", as Jean-Jaques Antier entitles his book (1991). Thus Guitton believes we are living in eschatological times, in which Genesis and Revelation hold the scriptural key. He notes that although Vatican II is relatively recent, the optimism of *Gaudium et Spes* is already rather *passé*, and that John Paul II did not speak like Paul VI. Everything is changing at an ever-increasing pace.

But Marthe was not involved with this change; she was living the Beatitudes in a darkened room without food, drink or sleep. Guitton remarks on the many people he has met in the course of his life who were incapable of beginning to understand why he believed in Christianity, and how difficult it is today for so many to accept an historic, datable religion. At the same time he notes the revival of interest in primary relics like the Shroud of Turin, and he compares Marthe with the Shroud, as a living testimony to the Passion of Christ.

If I have devoted so much space to Jean Guitton, it is because, of all that I have read on Marthe, he seems to me to have had the deepest insight into her character and significance; and in his book he has made some of the most profound comments about her.

8

Marcel Clément:
Philosopher and Journalist

Another philosopher who knew Marthe well over many years, and wrote a book about her, was Marcel Clément. He too was well-known in France and Canada in the twentieth century, and was the author of many books. His *Pour Entrer Chez Marthe* was published by Fayard.

Born in 1922, he managed to avoid being sent to work in a German labour camp during the Occupation. He first heard of Marthe in 1943 from a friend, François de la Noe, who worked with him in the Resistance Movement in Paris; but he didn't get to visit Châteauneuf until 1946, and then she was too ill to talk with him. He subsequently formed a relationship with her that lasted for 35 years, and he wrote his account of this in 1993.

The title of the book shows that in order to meet Marthe one had to enter her darkened room in an isolated farmhouse. But one had also to penetrate into the mystery that surrounded her to get close to her heart, which he tried to do over a long period of time. He made a total of 30 retreats at Châteauneuf under Fr Finet. While his professional life often took him abroad, he made his family home in the Drôme, and educated his children in the Foyer schools. He reckons he had about a hundred conversations with Marthe, and she had a profound influence on his life. Thus his witness is as cogent as that of Guitton.

Tens of thousands of visitors benefited directly from Marthe's warmth and light. Her life covered the greater part of the twentieth century, and, like Jean Guitton, Clément tries to place her and her influence in that turbulent and tragic period. He begins by pointing out that the situation in which she lived could hardly have been more inaccessible or hidden. When in 1950 he spoke of this to Fr Finet, the latter replied: "It's a test, you know. If it's genuine people will come; and if the influence lasts, there's a good chance that it may be serious." And Marthe's comment was: "It is in the desert that one finds God."

The Twentieth Century

The twentieth century witnessed an unparalleled demographic explosion, from one billion to six billion people. It also witnessed unprecedented technical and scientific progress, but also the most appalling wars and genocides. It saw the rise and fall of the first militant atheistic empire in history. Clément mentions the Paris Exhibition of 1900, and Expo '67 in Montreal, the Russian Revolution of 1917 and the fall of the Berlin wall in 1989. He also mentions the millions killed in wars, revolutions, ethnic cleansings, and by abortion. "Who can estimate the evil committed by mankind during this century?" And it was during that time that "the little peasant of the Drôme" was praying, suffering and shedding blood in the humble farmhouse at La Plaine. She was carrying on the work of Redemption initiated by Christ two thousand years before. Was it true, as Guitton had also quoted, that Jesus had told Marthe that she would be more closely united with His Passion than anyone since his Blessed Mother? (This was also quoted in the Special Number of *Alouette*, the Foyer Magazine, published just after her death). If so, her vocation in the fight against evil in the twentieth century was very special.

Marcel Clément visits Marthe

It was in 1943 that François de la Noe first talked to Clément about Marthe. Noe had managed to travel to Portugal, to meet Salazar the President, and Marthe was full of interest in their conversation about the Anglo-American landings in North Africa in 1942, and the possibility of a similar landing on the coast of France. The effect on Clément was to make him want to visit Marthe himself; it also caused him to read more books on the faith and to deepen his prayer life. From June 1944, the date of the landings in Normandy, he began to attend Mass daily. After the Surrender the following year, he was sent by the French government first to Calcutta, then to Indonesia, then to Japan, and finally to the USA, to help negotiate reparations for the damage inflicted by the Japanese in Indochina.

So it was that in May 1946 Clément and a friend called Jean Quesnal arrived at Châteauneuf to meet Fr Finet and Marthe. He had been warned that a meeting with Marthe might not be possible, since she had temporarily lost the power of speech. They travelled by train from St Valier, and walked up the hill to the Foyer, to be greeted by Mlle Martin who at the time was acting as secretary to both Fr Finet and Marthe. They were led to the study of "Le Père", where Finet gave them a summary of Marthe's background. He warned them against exaggerating the "extraordinary" in her life, but emphasised that her mission was to renew the Church in France, and that her suffering, united to that of Christ, would lead to this. He quoted the saying of St Paul in his letter to the Colossians, about making up in his body, for the Church, those things seen as lacking in the sufferings of Christ. He went on to explain the value of Marthe's suffering: "Members of his Mystical Body are called to share the Cross with Christ, to influence those who refuse to love or share the life of Christ." Clément remarked on the strength and youthfulness of Fr Finet—then aged 48; it was just ten years since his original meeting with Marthe. The new Foyer building next to the school was still not finished, and it was still the only Foyer. Yet Fr Finet told Clément with assurance: "The Lord promised Marthe that there would be Foyers in every continent. There will not be many in each country, but they will be world-wide."

Finet then drove them up to Marthe's farmhouse, where they waited in the kitchen. On entering Marthe's room Fr Finet said: "Let us kneel and say a prayer." Clément could just make out her head resting on a pillow; she was uttering regular groans. They prayed a decade of the rosary, and Fr Finet asked: "Have you any intentions to entrust to Marthe?" Having recently been in Saigon, all Clément could think of at that moment was to entrust the future of Indochina to her prayers. He never thought of mentioning personal intentions. Today there are three Foyers in Vietnam. As he walked back alone to the Foyer, he was suddenly overcome by emotion and burst into tears of joy. As we have seen, this was also the reaction of Yves de Boisredon, one of the last visitors to meet Marthe, in July 1980, and doubtless of many others too. At the Foyer he was greeted with the news that he was to leave for the USA at once. Fr Finet gave him a copy of the *True Devotion* by Blessed Louis de Montfort, (canonised the following year), saying: "You can read it on the plane." Thus he had met Marthe, but not yet spoken with her.

Marcel Clément's Vocation

Clément tells the story of how Fr Finet had found a copy of *The Secret of Mary* on Marthe's bed and how Our Lady had told her: "This is the book I would like to see spread throughout the world." Fr Finet said of her: "There was between Marthe and the Mother of Jesus an invisible intimacy, with frequent meetings." Today the spirituality of Grignion de Montfort lies behind many of the New Movements, even dating back to the time of the Legion of

Mary onwards, and John Paul II chose *Totus Tuus*—from St Louis's Marian consecration prayer—as his motto in 1978.

From May 1946 until November 1947 Marcel Clément was in Washington working with the French ambassador on the matter of Japanese reparations. There he tried to "empty himself of the spirit of the world, and fill himself with Jesus Christ through the Blessed Virgin Mary", as St Louis recommends. He attended Mass daily and took every opportunity of talking to his friends about Marthe. He corresponded with Fr Finet, and he made up his mind to return to Châteauneuf in the summer of 1947 to meet Marthe properly. This he did, and by chance arrived just as a retreat was starting. When he met Marthe a couple of days later her first words were, "so, the Blessed Virgin has brought you to make the retreat?" He came to realise how vital the Foyer retreat was in the scheme of things. Remember this was fifteen years before Vatican II, which he was to cover as a journalist, and he found that the essence of that important Ecumenical Council was anticipated by Fr Finet's retreats. For the first time, Clément really saw the mystery of God's love, which is transmitted to us in the Church. In his book he gives a graphic description of the retreat and his meeting with Marthe on the Thursday. He meditates on the fact that she would be starting to share Christ's Passion that evening as she did every week, and he contrasts that strange amalgam of matter-of-factness with mystical suffering that marked her life. He also notes the extraordinary fraternal charity he experienced at the conclusion of the retreat, when all were able to converse once more, having made their consecration to Jesus through Mary in the words of St Louis de Montfort.

Marcel Clément believed that his subsequent life was mapped out at that first conversation with Marthe. It had not gone according to his anticipated plan. She had initiated it entirely, and it had included talk about her goats and their veterinary problems! Towards the end she had hinted broadly that she thought his future lay in Canada, and she had asked him to keep in touch and send her news. Sure enough he decided to accept an offer from universities in Quebec and Montreal to join their faculties. This did not altogether please his father who had hoped his son might succeed him as a civil servant high up in the French Treasury. So it was, however, that Clément spent the next fifteen years teaching philosophy in Canadian universities. He recounts how his younger brother André, another gifted scholar, came under the spell of Châteauneuf and Marthe, and ended up in the philosophy faculties of Quebec and Montreal, much to their father's distress. He eventually finished up as Dean of the "Faculté Libre" in Paris.

The Role of the Laity

Clément has a chapter on the growing importance in the mission of the Church of the laity. This was one of the outcomes of Vatican II, and the Foyer movement played, and continues to play, a vital role in its development. The combination of Marthe, the lay woman, and Fr Finet, the priest, is essential to an understanding of both the Foyers and the relatively new lay apostolate. It was during the twentieth century that it became clear that every lay Christian has an apostolate; the term "priesthood of the laity" began to have a concrete meaning. Thus the Clément brothers were among the early apostles of the laity, with Marcel first as a university don and later as editor of the leading Catholic paper in France, *Homme Nouveau*. This was Fr Finet's principal message to the thousands of lay people who attended his retreats at Châteauneuf, that each one should become an apostle of Christ in the world.

And it is a message that has been repeated with growing insistence since Vatican II, in the face of an increasingly secular society. It is also true that in Great Britain it has had little effect, and critical comments are often made about the lack of formation given to the laity. Perhaps a Foyer or two might help! The situation is rather different in France, a country equally attacked by secularism, where there are no fewer than ten flourishing Foyers, with growing communities. It is to be hoped that the bishops of the UK will welcome this movement into their dioceses, as a positive move towards the proclaimed "Renewal of the Church", in the same way as the bishops of Africa are said to be doing. 1936 to 1981 was a period of crisis both for France and the Church. Marthe contributed not a little to the weathering of that crisis, from which certain parts of the Church are beginning to emerge in the early years of the twenty-first century.

Marthe and the Council

It is evident that what the Fathers of Vatican II were searching for in their efforts to make the Church a witness to the modern world was very much what Marthe and Fr Finet had in mind for the first Foyer. I would go so far as to say that, in my personal experience, I have found Vatican II interpreted at its best in the Foyers I have visited. Marcel Clément himself says in his book that during the Council, which he covered in Rome as a journalist, he felt himself entirely in agreement with the orientation that the Holy Spirit was giving to the Church, and that the "ensemble" of the council documents was in complete accord with the spirit of the Châteauneuf retreats.

For example, the liturgical innovations which followed the Council were anticipated at Châteauneuf in the fifties; the altar was moved forward and the priest faced the people. Readings were in French as well as in Latin; the "kiss of peace" was no mere formality. The Blessed Sacrament was reserved above a subsidiary altar on the right. An open Bible was placed on a lectern; the figure of Our Lady was prominent. New musical themes were introduced, and have been developed to suit the variety of Foyers in existence today. All this was done to try and make the Mass more meaningful for retreatants, and was prophetic, by twenty years, of the *Missa Normativa* introduced by Paul VI.

Another aspect of ecclesial life encouraged by the Council was a fresh ecumenical approach to non-Catholic Christians and those with no Christian faith. This too was normal practice in the Foyers, which welcomed any serious enquirer. Yet another aspect of Vatican II was the approach to countries living under the scourge of atheistic Communism, and the question of what was then called the "Conversion of Russia", for which every priest used to pray at the end of every Mass.

Marthe once said to Clément: "You know, it is all the suffering (of people in those countries) that will obtain the conversion of Russia", and he links this idea with the prophecies of Our Lady of Fatima, which indeed were to be at least partially fulfilled in the decade after Marthe's death. Since then the threat of Communism has been replaced by the reality of secularism under which so many people live as if God does not exist. The triumph of Our Lady's Immaculate Heart, foretold at Fatima in 1917, may seem as far away as ever, as does the "New Pentecost of Love" of which Marthe spoke. Yet there are encouraging signs which we must not ignore, nor must we lose hope as Benedict XVI has reminded us in his second encyclical letter *Spe Salvi*. According to Clément, Marthe said to him on several occasions: "We waste our time!", and the time wasted was not in some human effort but in prayer to God. The only way Christians will be able to resist the seduction of the secular world is by being more deeply united to God in prayer. "In the world you shall have distress: but have confidence, I have overcome the world," (Jn 16:33).

Clément argues that in the quarter century between the first retreat at Châteauneuf in 1936 and the opening of Vatican II in 1962, retreatants were receiving in practice all that was to come out of the Council—openness to the world, a renewal of the liturgy, the sense of the laity as the People of God, an understanding of the authority of the bishops united with the Pope, and the idea of a New Pentecost.

Marthe and the Assumption

In 1950, Pius XII proclaimed a Holy Year, and towards the end, (on November 1st), made the Assumption of Our Lady into Heaven a defined dogma of the Church. In St Peter's Square, before a huge crowd of faithful, on the Feast of All Saints, the Pope declared that the Mother of Jesus, Queen of all the Saints, had at the end of her life been assumed body and soul into Heaven.

In a letter to the parents of a young Canadian boy who was Marthe's godson but who had died the week before, Fr Finet wrote that he had been present in Rome for the promulgation of the new dogma, "which marked the culmination of Marthe's mission, who for many years had prayed and suffered for that grace." The letter is a remarkable document, if only because it reveals how certain she was that Our Lady gathered around her in Heaven the children who for whatever reason died young. This would in due course include the millions of aborted children. Fr Finet also mentions in his letter Communism, secularism, atheism and materialism, all of which deny that we return to God after we die. He closed the letter by visualising their little son in chivalric terms as Our Lady's Page.

Marcel Clément remarks of this letter that there are those who regret that Fr Finet did not keep more notes concerning Marthe's long life, but that those close to him were aware that he lacked time. In 1992, Fr Finet wrote to Clément to thank him for including the moving story of the death of Georges-Michel, Marthe's little godson, in his book.

He believes that the promulgation of the dogma by Pius XII was a crucial moment in modern times, and he compares Marthe's connection with this event to that of St Bernadette with the Immaculate Conception in 1858, so that just as the Blessed Virgin confirmed that dogma of 1854 in a private revelation to Bernadette Soubirous, so she confirmed the Dogma of the Assumption through Marthe. It must be left, of course, to the Church to pronounce on this, but it is a fascinating speculation. Clément witnessed Marthe sobbing bitter tears at the thought of Georges-Michel's death, because, like Christ weeping at the death of Lazarus, she was reacting in a human way. At the same time she was accorded a vision of the children around Mary in heaven, just as Our Lord knew that Lazarus would return to life. These mysteries are worth pondering, for they shed light on the Cross and suffering in general. Tears are a mark of love ... *sunt lacrimae rerum.* (The Latin phrase is from Virgil's *Aeneid* and speaks of tears for things which touch the soul). We too can experience natural distress and supernatural joy at the same time.

The Suicide of Henri Robin

In a moving chapter, Marcel Clément describes how he spent several hours with Marthe on 20 August 1951. It was shortly after the suicide of her brother Henri, and Fr Finet had only told him at the last minute. He found Marthe in floods of tears, and simply didn't know what to say to her. Twelve days had passed, and she was still distraught. Clément realised that Fr Finet had entrusted him with a delicate mission of consolation. Marthe stopped crying and told Clément what had happened. She drew his attention to a photo of Henri, which he looked at behind the curtain. "Il est beau, n'est-ce pas?" Marthe said; and Clément remarks that since then the word "beauté" has had a fresh meaning for him.

He recalls how he went to Lourdes in 1971 with a large pilgrimage of handicapped people, many of whom were born with Downs Syndrome and how "beautiful" they all were in the eyes of their parents: "Beauty is in the eyes of the beholder." Marthe spoke of Henri's funeral, and how in a way it had brought the local Christians and Republicans closer together. Little by little they talked of other things, of Canada, of the Foyer, and of Clément's latest book on the social doctrine of the Church. Finally he took his leave, saying that he thought Henri's extreme despair was a way of entrusting to Marthe's prayer all those in despair throughout the world. She remained silent, and they prayed together a Hail Mary. As he left the room she said: "Alors, à tous les jours..." which comes, in French, at the very end of Matthew's Gospel: "Lo, I am with you *always* [à tous les jours] even to the close of the age." Marthe's tears were indeed like those shed by Jesus over his friend Lazarus.

Marthe and her Passions

How easy it is to write: "Marthe relived the Passion, (of Christ), each week from October 1930 until her death in February 1981." To begin with she would come out of ecstasy on Saturday afternoon; in the forties it was on Sunday, and when Marcel Clément knew her it was on Monday afternoon—thus three and a half days. Does one ever get used to suffering? Once, when Clément thought he should leave Marthe because Fr Finet had told him she was particularly tired, he said: "I must leave you now; the Father said you were rather tired;" she replied: "But I am always tired."

Each Passion was a new experience; and in between she never slept; and her body—particularly her eyes—was subject to constant natural suffering. She may be said to have shared the redemptive suffering of Christ in a unique manner and to a unique degree. And yet to her visitors she appeared normal and even joyful. Clément knew her over a period of thirty-five years. He calculated he entered her room, alone or with Fr Finet, at least a hundred times. His testimony is therefore vital. And his constant impression was one of peace and joy. This peace and joy was transmitted in an extraordinary way to those who were privileged to meet her, if only for ten minutes. Thus from the Cross sprang the Resurrection.

The other impression that struck him forcibly was her amazing memory. As he says, she met about a hundred thousand visitors during her life, and corresponded with others, yet never seemed to forget either their names or their circumstances. The long period of time spent in ecstasy after each Passion in no way clouded the sharpness of her mind. Another feature emphasised by Clément is the way Marthe "felt with the Church" and was always completely submissive to its authority. As Pius XII was succeeded by John XXIII, then Paul VI, then briefly by John Paul I and finally by John Paul II, she upheld each in turn in her prayer.

The New Pentecost of Love

Clément recalls that in 1936, Marthe had spoken to Fr Finet about a "New Pentecost of Love" in the Church, and how twenty-three years later John XXIII had, on 10 May 1959, asked for prayers in order that "a new Pentecost might gladden the Christian family", as a week later he announced that the celebration of the forthcoming Ecumenical Council would be the occasion of a New Pentecost. Marthe saw Good Pope John not as a "caretaker Pope" but as the first pope in a new era of world history. She followed the course of the Council with close interest, and had many discussions with Clément, who covered it as a journalist. When Pope John died in June 1963 she prayed that Cardinal Montini would succeed him, as he did.

In August 1964, the weekly paper *Homme Nouveau*, for which Clément worked, published an article by Abbé Ricard encouraging the idea that the title "Mary Mother of the Church" should be given to Our Lady. This was exactly what Marthe wanted; and sure enough on 16 November, to the surprise of most to the bishops present, Pope Paul VI brought the session to a close by according to the Madonna the title *Mater Ecclesiae*. Four years later he issued his famous, if controversial, Encyclical *Humanae Vitae*, and Marthe was profoundly shocked at the subsequent attacks against the Holy Father. The last decade of her life was a time of crisis for the Church; in particular it was a period of crisis in the lives of many priests, and many are the testimonies of priests who were helped by Marthe.

Marthe and the Bishops of Valence

Marcel Clément has a chapter exploring the relationship of Marthe and Fr Finet with the bishops of Valence. First came Mgr Pic from 1932 to 1953; it was he who insisted on the medical examination conducted by the two doctors from Lyon in 1942, and who watched over the early growth of the Foyer in a friendly way. He blessed the new building in 1948. He was followed by Mgr Urtasun, who took both of them to his heart, and who helped organise the twenty-fifth Anniversary of the Foyer, before being promoted to become Archbishop of Avignon. This happened in 1961 in some style, presided over by the Cardinal Archbishop of Lyon. By then the local bishop was Mgr Vignancourt, who made Fr Finet, who was already a Canon of Lyon, a Canon of Valence! He too became an archbishop, and was succeeded at Valence by Mgr de Canbourg. He only lasted a short while, and was succeeded in 1978 by Mgr Marchand, who conducted Marthe's funeral in 1981, at which the Foyer Fathers from twenty-five countries were present. By this time Marthe's Foyers were in every continent of the world. She was indeed a "Daughter of the Church."

Thoughts about Marthe

Clément gives a number of examples of Marthe's prudence in the advice she gave to her visitors. She was always practical and generally left decisions to her enquirers. She often asked searching questions that helped resolve problems. Once she hinted to him that any work fruitful for God must involve suffering. In the fifties, he wished to entitle one of his books *The Art of Loving;* "Oh no," said Marthe, "I would prefer *The Joy of Loving.*" It duly went into several editions in Canada and in France. He mentions, too, how Marthe and Fr Finet did everything they could to avoid allowing journalists to publish anything on her. *Homme Nouveau* never mentioned her until after her death.

Marcel Clément tries to analyse the effect that her weekly "Passions" had on Marthe. He experienced many conversations with her, both before and after. In an illuminating sentence he says that he never spotted a trace in her of any attitude not based on faith, hope and charity. He remarks too on her capacity to keep silence—her silences were remembered later as even more evocative than her words. She never said anything unnecessary, and weighed her words carefully. Clément contrasts what she wrote (or dictated) as a young woman with her conversation in later life, and writes: "Marthe never ceased to grow in stature." Her evident wisdom, increasing with maturity, was based on firm foundations.

Her prayer was constant. Père Raymond Peyret entitled his 1985 book *Prends ma Vie, Seigneur: La Longue Messe de Marthe Robin*. She never attended Mass after 1928, yet her life was one constant offering to the Father in union with the Son. It is significant that the prayer she and Fr Finet, and other privileged visitors, prayed on Thursday evenings was the Rosary. Our Lady was never far away. Marthe received her weekly Communion on Wednesday evening, and then spent the night in ecstasy; Clément remarks that these were the only hours each week when she did not suffer. The fruit of Marthe's offering was to be seen in the retreats given by Fr Finet, and later by other priests. On two occasions he allowed Clément to see Marthe after her Passion, and with a small torch illuminated the blood on her forehead and cheeks. They then walked back to the Foyer to pray in the chapel, filled with the friendship of the Lord transmitted through Marthe ... "a friendship vaster than human intelligence, and larger than the human heart!"

"Do you want to be like Me?"

In a chapter headed *Veux-tu être comme Moi?* Clément examines the mystery of Marthe's stigmata. Any number of visitors, himself included, testified to having seen both coagulated and fresh blood on her forehead, and tears stained with blood issuing from her eyes. Less visible, of course, were the other marks of the Crucifixion. As, we have seen, in 1942 two leading doctors from Lyon, Drs Dechaume and Ricard were asked by the bishop to make a detailed medical examination of Marthe, which is preserved in a document 35 pages long, and Clément quotes parts of this. They apparently concluded that she was suffering from a form of encephalitis, an inflammatory disorder of the brain.

What is interesting is that, having washed the blood from her various "wounds" they could find no lesions on her skin. Thus, to deepen the mystery, they testify both to the abundance of blood and to the absence of lesions. Their conclusion was that in the present state of medical knowledge they could see neither the cause not the mechanism for these stigmata.

The description of what happened in October 1930, given by Marthe to Fr Finet and quoted in the Special Number of *Alouette*, (August 1981), in no way contradicted this medical evidence. Clément quotes St John of the Cross, St Francis de Sales, and St Bonaventure—all Doctors of the Church—who commented on the stigmata of St Francis of Assisi in 1224. All agree that this apparent miracle is a sign of God's special favour, and that the wounds of Christ mark the soul as much as the body.

Marthe's Mission in the Church

So what was Marthe's mission? Clément points out the immense changes that have occurred in the world since 1930. Hitler had not yet come to power in Germany, and a second world war seemed almost unimaginable. The Vatican State had only just regained its independence. News and information still travelled relatively slowly. Communism was still restricted to Russia. John XXIII would be the first pope to leave Rome in the twentieth century and that was to take a train to Assisi! Air travel was in its infancy, and the internet was not even dreamt of. The atom had only just begun to give up its secrets, and DNA was unknown. And there in an isolated village in a remote part of France was a handicapped farmer's daughter who had been entrusted by God with a mission to the world. For the next fifty years He was to reveal its nature to her, and the first Foyer was to be emulated by many others in every part of the globe. Their communities were to recapture the spirit of the earliest Christian communities of whom it was said: "See how they love one another." All of this was hidden in 1930.

Marcel Clément repeats the famous account of the prophecy given by Jesus to Marthe in 1933, and published in the Special Edition of *Alouette* of 1981. It was this that she passed on to Fr Finet at their first meeting on 10 February 1936, and much of which was incorporated into the Statutes of the Foyers of Charity which were submitted to Rome in the late eighties. And all was to be fulfilled in the many communities founded from Châteauneuf.

For ten years Fr Finet had to divide his time between Châteauneuf and his old diocese of Lyon, and he would preach about seven retreats a year. As we have seen, Marie-Ange Dumas and Hélène Fagot attended the original retreat in September 1936, and then took charge of the school, as little by little the community grew. In 1953, the Boys' school was started at Saint-Bonnet, and during that decade about ten new Foyers were founded. Columbia welcomed the first overseas foundation, followed by Africa and Canada. Since then the development has been steady, the one exception being the Anglophone world. Such an expansion can only be explained as an act of God, backed by the prayer and sacrifice of Marthe Robin.

Like Marthe herself, the spirituality of the Foyers is based firmly on devotion to the Eucharist, devotion to the Blessed Virgin, and loyalty to the Magisterium of the Church. The extraordinary life of Marthe enthuses all this human effort. The three evangelical virtues of poverty, chastity and obedience are in evidence, as well as light, charity and love. It may not be far-fetched to say that this is a new form of religious life; and a friend of mine who was torn between a vocation to a Foyer and one to the Carmelite life—which in the end she followed—told me they were equally demanding. But life in a Foyer is more adapted to modern living, and vocations to their communities are more numerous.

The spirituality of St Louis de Montfort was certainly one of the strongest influences on both Marthe's life and that of Fr Finet; Mary, whom she referred to as *maman chérie*, was never far from her mind. The other big influence was Carmel and St Thérèse. Early in her life she had been attracted to the idea of the Carmelite cloister, and then the visions of 1926 had put her firmly into the Little Way of Spiritual Childhood and had even given her the role of continuing the work of that great saint. It is true that Marthe was enrolled in the Third Order of St Francis in 1928 by the parish missioners, but there seems to have been no Third Order of Mount Carmel in her neck of the woods. The love shown to so many by Marthe was very like that practised by Thérèse Martin.

The Death of Marthe

Clément says that, seeing how many times Marthe experienced a mystical death in her Passions, one might reasonably have supposed that her actual death would be a peaceful one. But it was not to be. She was found by Fr Finet dead on the floor beside her divan on the evening of Friday 6th February 1981; her room was in unnatural disorder. The only explanation could be that her spiritual enemy, who had attacked her physically on so many occasions, was allowed to eject her from her bed. All those who knew her say that there could be no question of her getting out of bed on her own. She had been totally immobile for decades, and had no "natural functions" to cause her to leave her bed. Marthe's death remains shrouded in mystery, like so much of her life. We know that she looked forward to death as the gateway to eternal life and the end of her earthly suffering. The real mystery is the length of time God accorded her on earth. She was nearly seventy-nine years old at the time of her death. In 1930, at a time when she expressed much of her most profound thought, she had said: "I surprise people when I say I live to die, and that death is the great idea, the very meaning of my life. Death is the grace of all graces, and the crown of our Christian life ... it is our complete fulfilment in love. It completes our possession of divine life," (3 January 1930). Nevertheless it seems that her death came as a surprise to Fr Finet and the members of her community.

The last letter received by Clément was dated 4 September 1980, and was to thank him for the book he had recently sent to Marthe. Clément sent her a copy of all his books as they appeared. The letter was of course dictated, and it showed that she had read it and "taken it on board". No one suspected that five months later she would be dead. He points out that the death of Jesus, Peter, and so many of the early saints was far from peaceful, and Marthe's violent end places her amongst the greatest Christians. Like her Master she was completely humiliated at the end, literally thrown to the ground (*humus*). Thus was her link with the Cross of Jesus sealed. Even the date was significant, for she was called to her reward just halfway through the novena that she kept each year from the Feast of the Purification until the anniversary of the first apparition at Lourdes. Many friends of the Foyers observed that novena. It was four days before the forty-fifth anniversary of the first meeting between Marthe and Fr Finet, and also a First Friday.

Next morning, the First Saturday, Fr Finet announced her death to the media and to all the Foyers worldwide. The newspapers, radio and television gave the event considerable publicity. On Tuesday the 10th Marthe's body was taken from the farmhouse where she had spent her entire life, to the sanctuary of the new chapel, and two days later Mgr Marchand conducted her funeral Mass, attended by many thousands of her friends. She was buried in the family vault at Saint-Bonnet. Five years later her cause was opened at Valence, and since 1995 has been dealt with at Rome.

Let us conclude this chapter with the prayer she composed in 1930: "Lord Jesus, You have promised that when I leave this earth, I shall go directly to join You. When I am with You I shall see to the sinners of the whole world, until the end of the world. And I shall have a particular concern for all the friends of the Foyers of Charity, those I have known during my life, and all those who will come later. I shall keep watch over them all in a special way, but always discretely. I shall constantly help them, without their realising it; yes, I shall always be with them!" This was a wonderful forecast, written six years before the foundation of the first Foyer.

9

Les Trois Sagesses of
Père Marie-Dominique Philippe OP

Published in 1994, this book took the form of interviews between Frédéric Lenoir and Fr Marie-Dominique Philippe on the three sources of wisdom—philosophy, theology, and mysticism. In the third section on Mysticism, the influence of Marthe Robin on Père Philippe and his Community of St John is discussed in great depth. I shall now use some of the insights revealed here, which, like those of Jean Guitton and Marcel Clément, throw light on the subject of this book.

First some words on the life of Père Philippe. He was born near the beginning of the twentieth century, and became a Dominican in 1930, much influenced by his uncle, Père Dehau OP. Ordained priest in 1936, he specialised in philosophy, and after the war was appointed a professor of philosophy at the international University of Fribourg in Switzerland. It was from there that he first met Marthe, in 1947, and twenty-five years later he was asked by some of his students if he would found a new congregation in which they could live a religious life. There were five who were determined to stay with Père Philippe.

But he was already over 60, and very doubtful if this was God's will for him and for them. To begin with he made enquiries whether he might integrate them into an existing order. He had contacts with the Cistercians at Lerins, the island off the coast at Nice where St Augustine and his forty companions had paused on their way to Britain in 597. At the same time he went to consult Marthe at Châteauneuf, where he had preached retreats in the Foyer for many years. She gave him the green light with the words, "Father, this comes from the Holy Spirit. You must listen to the appeal of your students—it is Jesus who is asking you. Do whatever you can for them."

Fr Marie-Dominique said: "If Marthe had discouraged me, I would have dropped the idea. I would have sent them back to their various dioceses." However, a cardinal and four bishops also encouraged him to start a new congregation. Very quickly Rome approved his "Community of St John", which started in a house in Fribourg. Fr Marie-Dominique continued to live with his Dominicans, but visited his students frequently. Given a free choice, he tells us, he would gladly have retired from the university to have more time for contemplation and prayer. As it was, he became increasingly involved with his Order, which grew in an astonishing way. He wrote a Rule for these young men that the Bishop of Toulon said was just what was needed today. The Benedictine link with Lerins was useful too.

The Community of St John

As the Order grew, and as it trained its priests, there were accusations that they were creating a parallel clergy, that they were traditionalists in league with Mgr Lefebvre, and other absurd calumnies. Some bishops treated them with suspicion to start with, and some nasty anonymous letters were circulated. It is true that many French seminaries were going through a difficult time, as in the US, but Fr Marie-Dominique's aim was not to challenge them. He simply gave his members the best spiritual formation that he knew. As time went on, and as John Paul II's reign progressed, they became not only accepted, but were invited into more and more dioceses to take over parishes. The fact that these young men and women chose to wear a habit was considered odd by the liberals, but this did not come from their founder. Fr Marie-Dominique remained profoundly Dominican, while encouraging students to join his new community. There was thus a real link between his new foundation and the more traditional orders of St Dominic and St Benedict. In the early days, Marthe encouraged Fr Marie-Dominique to accept as many applications as he could, and the community grew remarkably; but inevitably not all turned out to be suitable. The formation given to these young applicants was second to none, both in philosophy and theology.

At the beginning of the section called "Sagesse Mystique," Fr Marie-Dominique explains at length why his new community is founded on the teaching of St John, author of the fourth Gospel and the Book of Revelation. He linked this with the essential Marian aspect of their devotion: "The mystery of John is for the whole Church, and not just for our community." St Thomas Aquinas gives three reasons why he believed that Jesus loved John even more than Peter: his intelligence, his purity of heart, and his youth. Fr Marie-Dominique insists that John was the author of the fourth Gospel, a fact which has been challenged by many modern scholars. He is convinced, too, that Mary had a huge influence on John since they were together at the foot of the Cross, and thereafter lived together: "Son, behold thy Mother."

Fr Marie-Dominique finds significance in the five meals mentioned in St John's Gospel. The first is the Wedding Feast at Cana; the second, the occasion when Jesus multiplied the loaves; the third, the meal at Bethany with Mary and Martha; the fourth, the Last Supper when Jesus washed his disciples' feet; and the fifth, the early morning breakfast by the Lake of Galilee. Just as the Old Testament is punctuated by sacrifices, so the final gospel is punctuated by meals. And Meals represent the mystery of fraternal charity.

The Wisdom of the Cross and Marthe Robin

The mystery of the suffering endured by Jesus in his Passion will always remain for us a source of scandal and folly. His Mother Mary shared it with him, and so did St John. For them, too, the Cross was a mystery so deep and dark it defies human understanding. At the same time they accepted it (as St Paul says in 1 Cor 1:24) as the wisdom of God. If, as Jesus said, the greatest manifestation of love is to lay down one's life for one's friends, then the Cross becomes supremely meaningful. Thus the Cross shows both Jesus' love for mankind and the glorification of his Father in Heaven. This is the significance of what we call "sacrifice," a theme that we now associate with the Mass. St Luke clearly associates Christ's Passion with his prayer to the Father, and so we may assume that he derived his information from St John, just as he derived so much from Our Lady. And the "cup of suffering" that Our Lord prayed in the Garden might be spared him is one that his Mother, and John and Mary of Magdala, and each one of us, have to share with him. The Father desires that all his Son's followers accept a share in His sufferings; this is the mystery of com-passion.

All of which leads us to Marthe Robin, who shared in Jesus' Passion to a far greater extent than most other Christians. Fr Marie-Dominique first heard of Marthe from Père Eberhardt, who founded the Foyer at Poissy near Paris in the 'fifties. He was an outstanding priest, known as "God's bulldozer." These two priests were about the same age. Fr Marie-Dominique was a little suspicious of stigmatists, and did not want to meet Marthe initially. It was she who heard of him being at Fribourg, and through a retreatant invited him to visit her. So he came to La Plaine in September 1948, and spent a whole hour with her alone. She spoke about his uncle, Père Dehau, who had greatly influenced his youth, and had been his first spiritual father. She spoke of him as of an old friend, though she had never met him; this greatly impressed

Fr Marie-Dominique. When he came to leave her, she asked for his blessing, as she always did of priests, and she asked him to pray for her. He received a strong impression of an important link in the Mystical Body, of which he became increasingly conscious. But he returned to Fribourg uncertain as to whether he would ever see her again.

Sixteen years passed; and then quite suddenly he received a telephone call from Fr Finet asking him whether he would care to preach a retreat for priests at Châteauneuf. He accepted at once, and in 1964 he returned to the Foyer to lead the retreat and to meet Marthe for the second time. He took as his theme the Gospel of St John, and in those days there were four one hour conferences each day. Talking to the retreatants on the last day Fr Finet said: "When I told Marthe that Fr Marie-Dominique was to preach this retreat to priests, she simply said: 'Enfin!' " (At last!). Fr Marie-Dominique came to realise how much Marthe was centred on St John. "She was a child of the Father, a child of the Virgin Mary, and a child of Jesus Crucified ..."

Marthe and St Thérèse

He understood, too, how closely linked Marthe was with St Thérèse and the Carmelites. More than once he heard her say: "The Foyers should be like little Carmels, places of silence and prayer and welcome." She was all in favour of the religious life, and following the evangelical counsels. What counted above all, though, was total consecration to God through Mary. "Through the eyes of God's Wisdom, Thérèse and Marthe are inseparable. Marthe 'achieved' Thérèse's act of offering, sharing in the sufferings of the Cross. Marthe was the victim of Love." St Thérèse was called by the Church "Patroness of the Missions," and Marthe carried on this work. The mystery of Marthe was similar to that of St Thérèse; a perfect imitation of the sacrificial offering of Mary. Both were completely identified with her. As St Louis de Montfort put it in *The Secret of Mary*: "It is Mary who lives in the (consecrated) soul." Fr Marie-Dominique wrote: "I myself tried to live the mystery of Marthe, which obliged me to go always deeper into interiority and silence."

Fr Marie-Dominique points out that whereas St Thérèse lived for less than twenty-five years, Marthe's life went on for a long time, covering indeed more than three-quarters of the twentieth century. Both were profoundly linked with Jesus crucified through his Mother. And Marthe was profoundly linked with St Louis de Montfort, whose "consecration to Jesus through Mary" concludes every Foyer Retreat. Fr Finet once said to Fr Marie-Dominique: "It is here (to Châteauneuf) that the Blessed Virgin comes most often," and he was not surprised. Mary watched over this infirm child, who lay on her divan as if in her mother's womb.

If Fr Marie-Dominique had to preach at a Mass when a new Foyer member was to be received, he always consulted Marthe first, to ensure that what he was going to say was in the spirit of the Foyers; and on one occasion Marthe remarked: "You have understood perfectly the mystery of the Foyers, the source of which is Mary." And whenever he preached a retreat at Châteauneuf, he was very conscious that both he and the retreatants were upheld by Marthe's prayer. Leading a retreat for priests was particularly onerous, but he always found the experience rewarding. Marthe loved priests so much, and Fr Finet told him that she suffered especially during their retreats. They would return from their visit to Marthe, "like children who had been to see their mother", for she gave them fresh hope. She never, however, gave them positive directions; these were left to their superiors or to the preacher.

Marthe's Simplicity and Directness

When Fr Marie-Dominique had his private sessions with Marthe, he found he could talk with her about anything with complete simplicity. "One had the impression of a direct contact with Jesus, with Mary, with Heaven and with the

Father." He tells us that at his first retreat he said to Marthe: "I should love to come and pray beside you when you are having one of your Passions," to which she replied: "That's entirely up to the Father." But later, on Thursday, Fr Finet, who was following the retreat, said to Fr Marie-Dominique: "Marthe has asked that you come with me tomorrow when she is experiencing her Passion. She would also like to hear a recording of your conducted Rosary." Thus he was able, on occasion, over the course of seventeen years, to take Holy Communion to Marthe on Wednesday evenings, and pray for ten minutes during her Passions on Fridays. He recounts how she longed to enter more deeply into this mystery every week, yet it became increasingly painful for her. Her life was a struggle on behalf of the whole Church, and it got no easier as she grew older.

He makes another interesting remark at this point, namely that Marthe had a passion for intellectual precision which he, as a philosopher, found astonishing; she was always sensitive to precision in language and the meaning of words. She had a thirst for truth. When sometimes she praised what he had said in his retreat conferences (which would be read to her) he had the impression that she had been mystically present. "I believe that Marthe, in that she truly carried on the mystery of the little Thérèse, has been given to the Church to help in its great struggle in the times in which we live."

Marthe always expressed her opinions with great delicacy. But she was capable of being critical of even well-known theologians. Fr Marie-Dominique gives the example told to him by Fr Finet of how, soon after the war, she had reproved the notable Dominican Fr Garrigou-Lagrange for not writing a book on Our Lady. When in due course he did write this work, which was read to Marthe, she remarked that he could have done it better. Another example of her direct approach concerned a young man on retreat whose girl-friend was pregnant. He told Marthe, and wondered whether he should marry the lady. Her reply was: "One does not build a marriage on sin. Have the courage to follow your actions to their conclusion. Wait until the child is born; then you will see whether she can be your wife. You should be in no hurry."

But on the whole Marthe was always positive and very rarely critical. "And I, if I be lifted up from the earth, will draw all things to myself." (Jn 12:32) "What struck one most forcibly was the way Marthe was drawn to Jesus, in the greatest poverty. When one went to see her, one found her on the threshold of Heaven. One felt in the presence of someone who lived the whole time with Jesus and Mary. At the same time she was completely united with her visitors. And when one thinks of the number of people she met every week..."

Marthe's Sufferings

Marthe's suffering can only be understood in the light of that of Christ in his Passion. It is a deep mystery, but it is linked with the suffering of so many people in their day-to-day lives. Every visitor was greeted as if he or she was the most important one that day. Human psychology hardly came into the picture; it was God alone who mattered; one felt one was in direct relation with her, and through her with Jesus and Mary. But not everyone was able to benefit from their meeting with Marthe, and some invented falsehoods later. Fr Marie-Dominique recounts many anecdotes that bring Marthe to life, and which show how she adapted her response to each individual. "Whenever I was with Marthe, I felt that time no longer existed; I was in the presence of someone who was a witness of eternity, a witness of God's eternal love for us, and of Mary's tenderness of heart."

Asked about Marthe's concern for the children killed by abortion, and the link between her life and the mystery of the Holy Innocents of Bethlehem, Fr Marie-Dominique replied: "Marthe's whole life was a holocaust, from 1930 to 1981. Whereas the Holy Innocents had no choice in their martyrdom, Marthe's life was inspired (as all those who knew her will testify) by an amazing lucidity, deeply marked by suffering, and purified by love for Our Lord. Yet there was something common to both. Marthe's acceptance of her condition had an element of 'radical passivity'. Medically speaking she should not have been alive; God alone sustained her. Her holiness consisted in total abandonment to the hands of her Father. I cannot see that her abandonment could have been more complete. And the more she lived this state, the more the devil attacked her; right to the end she maintained this combat in solitude. This mystery of abandonment is even deeper than that of her suffering, and can only be explained in relation to Christ's abandonment on the Cross. 'Father, into your hands...' It was very similar to that of St Thérèse."

Marthe's Voice

Fr Marie-Dominique received an insight into Marthe's character still more profound than those of Jean Guitton and Marcel Clément. Replying to Frédéric Lenoir, he emphasises Marthe's incredible joy, despite her handicap and suffering, that was revealed chiefly in her voice. "One could write a whole book on Marthe's voice." He compares it to a limpid spring of water. True she could laugh and smile; but it was with her voice that she revealed the fervour of her love for Jesus and for whoever happened to be with her. She showed a joy that came from the heart of a child in the presence of its Father. The joys of Mary are to be found in all the mysteries of her Rosary, even in the Sorrowful ones. And Marthe had such a sense of humour. It enabled her to be totally tolerant of things of which she disapproved, and quite non-judgemental of people's failings. Her amazing intelligence, so logically penetrating, was always spiced with love and humour.

Towards the late seventies, so Fr Marie-Dominique tells us, Marthe suffered some "dark nights," just like St Thérèse and Blessed Mother Teresa of Calcutta. We know that Fr Finet and the Foyer organisation were facing something of a crisis. One day, Marthe confided in Fr Marie-Dominique that she felt useless, and that it might be better if she left Châteauneuf. "Take me away to a loony-bin", she said! On that occasion she was helped by the visit of some new recruits to the Foyer. On another occasion, when Fr Marie-Dominique was alone with her, she suddenly said: "Father, when is he going to come?" He thought she was referring to Fr Finet, and replied he would go and get him. "No, Father, I mean Jesus ... when is He going to come for me?" She was longing to leave the earth. The final words of the New Testament are: "I am coming soon ... come Lord Jesus." In the event He came on 6 February 1981.

The Mystery of the Sepulchre

Fr Marie-Dominique's final chapter in *Les Trois Sagesses* is an in-depth meditation on the two days that Holy Scripture tells us Jesus spent in the tomb of Joseph of Arimathea, between his death on Good Friday and his Resurrection on "the first day of the week", which we now call Easter Sunday. In the Apostles' Creed we say, "He descended into Hell," (though this is not mentioned in the Nicene Creed), and the tradition of the Fathers is that He preached to the souls in Sheol or Hades, that is the abode of the dead, and that, in the words of the *Catechism*, (633), he went to "free the just who had gone before him." Fr Marie-Dominique believed this to be an important mystery, and that Marthe shared in it more than most holy people.

He lays great stress on the fragility of Marthe's body. Biologically she was cut off from all that makes normal humans enjoy life, and so should have died. She could not eat or drink, she could not sleep, she could not enjoy sunshine; and she shed blood constantly through the stigmata she received in 1930. Thus she lived for half a century in a sort of sepulchre. This prolonged miracle can only be explained as due to the direct action of God. He speaks of her death in so violent a manner as "the great mystery of Marthe's death." He also stresses her complete obedience to her spiritual Father.

Just as the Word made Flesh lay for two days inanimate in the sepulchre, so the body of Marthe lay for half a century on the little divan in her room at the farmhouse, apparently inanimate yet actually filled with the Spirit of Christ. She was a unique combination of flesh and spirit.

Marthe's Intelligence and Humility

She was also endowed with exceptional intelligence. "I have rarely come across anyone as intelligent as Marthe", says Fr Marie-Dominique. When she put theological questions to him, it was with a precision and rigour of thought that amazed him. At the same time she showed a great warmth of heart, and an exceptional sense of mercy; to all who came to see her she gave hope and confidence. Fr Marie-Dominique speaks frequently of her stigmata in his final chapter, and he believed that she went beyond most others marked with the wounds of Christ, by living the Mystery of the Sepulchre, and by the charism of compassion that she showed so clearly. "I am sure that by looking deeply at the mystery of compassion in her last achievement—the Mystery of the Sepulchre—one will understand a great many facts in the life of Marthe ... she was in a state of ultimate humility. It seems to me that it is a mystery reserved for the Church in the end-times. St Paul anticipates it in his Letter to the Philippians (chapter 2)."

In the littleness that she shared with St Thérèse, and in complete humility and poverty, she lived through an age of suffering for the Church in anticipation of a New Pentecost of Love. The strength to do this was derived from both Jesus and Mary, who together shared the joys and sufferings of the human condition. In this way Marthe brings all those who know her into the closest communion with the Incarnation.

Marthe's Legacy: A Summing up

Not for nothing did Marthe's life cover most of the twentieth century. She lived both before and after the Vatican Council, and was prophetically a source of grace to those who wished to understand that Council, and the renewal that it meant to bring to the Church and the world. The charism brought to the twentieth century by St Thérèse has already been fully recognised and approved by the Church. Let us hope that the charism which developed from the life and witness of Marthe may be fully appreciated and approved in the twenty-first century. Fr Marie-Dominique explains how difficult it was for some Catholics to accept the real meaning of the Council. Many were misled into the deviations of progressivism or traditionalism. To escape these errors one needed the love and trust of a child in its mother's womb, and of this Marthe was a complete witness. She represented all that was best in the deliberations and documents which came from the Council. "I am convinced that Marthe represents something final."

Yet it is not easy to enter fully into what Marthe, under the influence of the Holy Spirit and in dependence on Mary, wanted to transmit to us, and still wants to transmit. For though we can no longer consult her at Châteauneuf, we can approach her interiorly, and without moving from where we happen to be. Just as St Joan of Arc had the voices of St Catherine and St Margaret to guide her, so we can seek the guidance of Marthe. But we must bear in mind that she never claimed to foresee the future. Again and again she responded to people's questions and suggestions with silence; with the result that some rationalists have failed to understand her, and often she has been misrepresented.

Marthe as an instrument of God

If the Church has to experience the Mystery of the Sepulchre, as did Mary, we may understand that in Marthe God has given us a sign, and a very important sign. That is why Fr Marie-Dominique insists on the importance of the connection between Marthe and the Community of St John. In the end it is only love and mercy that count, as we prepare for the Second Coming of Jesus. "For me Marthe was an instrument of God." Many saints have shared the Cross of Jesus; but Marthe shared His Sepulchre to a greater degree than most. If it is God's will that the Church undergoes a period of "experiencing the Sepulchre," then Marthe will be a key figure. The Resurrection comes mysteriously from the tomb, as Jesus' inanimate body emerges to take on new life, and in the same way will come the revival of the Church. Marthe may well represent something final (*ultime*) in the divine economy. Her self-offering in poverty, silence, and complete abandonment to the will of God, were of an unusual if not unique order.

Fr Marie-Dominique saw in Paul VI's proclamation of Mary as the Mother of the Church, at the conclusion of Vatican II, a significant sign. It seems that he had hesitated, and was then shown a text from one of the Fathers of the Church that suggested that, while the body of Christ lay in the Sepulchre, the whole faith of the Church had found refuge in the Heart of his Mother. This text convinced him. Mary is the guardian of the Church's faith for all time. And Marthe's life bears witness to this fact. We may recall, too, that Marthe had prayed especially for this proclamation during the Council. When asked by Frédéric Lenoir what he thought Marthe meant by a "New Pentecost of Love," Fr Marie-Dominique replied that she meant there would be a renewal of the Church in the world, and that the Foyers were already witnessing to this. Marthe herself prepared for this renewal, notably by supporting the Council in her prayer.

And he stresses how she was always an advocate of sound doctrine, because she had a passion for truth. The Foyers were to manifest "light, charity and love", and the light was to bring sound teaching to God's people. This was at a time when sound teaching was often lacking. Some have objected that charity and love are virtually the same thing. Marthe herself once explained that charity implied fraternal charity among Christians, whereas love concerned chiefly God the Father, in contemplation. It's all there in St John's first

Epistle. Thus the Foyers and the Community of St John are closely linked in their spirituality, and both go back to the sources of religious life, that is to say to the Virgin Mary in her total consecration to God. And Marthe greatly admired what Fr Marie-Dominique brought to the Foyers, that is the three wisdoms of philosophy, theology and mysticism that ordered their lives.

10

Marthe and the
New Ecclesial Communities

It has been generally agreed for two thousand years that
ideally to follow Christ presupposes living in community with
other Christians. There are individuals who have found their
vocation to live alone as hermits, but, as St Benedict taught,
this should only happen after an apprenticeship in
community. The basic and most widespread community in
society is, of course, the family. Few families, however, are
normally self-sufficient; and when the state decrees that no
married couple shall have more than one child—as is the case
for certain segments of the population in modern China—it
means that three people are a somewhat limited community.
Throughout the history of the Church, Christians have
sought to live in community, and indeed what St Luke
describes in the first chapter of the Acts of the Apostles is a
kind of template of community life.

In the twentieth century, and particularly after Vatican II,
we observe two trends: first the established religious
communities such as the Jesuits and Benedictines saw a
decline in vocations; and second, numerous new
communities, made up largely of lay persons, have emerged.
Some observers, like Fr Ian Ker, the Newman Scholar, have
seen this as providential, and believe that the new

communities are God's instruments for reviving the Church and giving it a new orientation. In this section I shall look at those new communities that originated in France, and on which Marthe Robin had an influence.

Communities and Movements influenced by Marthe

The first, of course, was the Foyer of Charity movement that began in 1936. The second, according to Raymond Peyret, was called "The Little Sisters of Jesus", and was founded in 1939 by Sr Magdalen, who met Marthe for the first time in 1943, and who visited her regularly thereafter. When Marthe died in 1981, Sr Magdalen recalled the deep affection that existed between them, and how much Marthe had encouraged her in her work of propagating the memory and aims of Blessed Charles de Foucauld, who died in 1916. In 1946, Thérèse Cornille founded another new movement that she called "Foyers Claire Amitié", and two years later she met Marthe with whom she formed a deep friendship. Her work was mainly among young people in deprived areas. The community grew, and in due course spread from France to Africa, and Cambodia. When serious trouble erupted in that country, Marthe assured her that none of her members would be lost, and sure enough all were repatriated. This was yet another example of Marthe carrying on the work of St Thérèse in the mission field.

In 1944, a Père Talvas founded a movement that he called "The Nest". Prostitution was on the increase during the Occupation, and the Nests were places of refuge for women who wished to escape from that form of slavery. Starting in the big French cities, they later spread to Portugal and thence to Brazil. In 1949, Père Talvas met Marthe and questioned her about the future of his work. He was struck by her good sense and her perspicacity. She recommended to him *Le Secret de Marie* by St Louis de Montfort. Talvas also got to know Jean Guitton. Another new community, but not of French origin, that is associated with Marthe is the Focolari. This was started in Italy during World War II by Chiara Lubich, who never actually met Marthe, though several of her associates did around 1962. One of them said later: "We had the impression of a saint, a great saint, and she brought to us some splendid fruit." Perhaps more famous was L'Arche, ("The Ark"), the movement founded by Jean Vanier in 1964. These were and are communities of persons with learning disabilities who are looked after by dedicated carers. In 1976, quite late in Marthe's life, Vanier went on a retreat to Châteauneuf, and met Marthe. She had known about the Arks for a long time and carried them in her prayer. Certain Foyers specialise in retreats for the disabled to this day.

Mary Doohan's "Little Way Association" in England is undoubtedly linked with Marthe's apostolate. There was a physical link in India. Her work in the second half of the twentieth century was to raise money to support missionary ventures, under the guidance and inspiration of the Little Flower who with St Francis Xavier was proclaimed a Patron of the Missions.

Marthe and Vatican II

Writing in praise of the Second Vatican Council and its splendid documents, Bishop Patrick O'Donoghue of Lancaster—whose challenging 2008 study, *Fit for Mission? Church*, was frankly critical of much that has happened to the Church in England and Wales since the Council—wrote in the *Catholic Herald* (25 January 2009): "Looking back across the years, we are prone to forget, or dismiss as naïve, the sheer energy and hope of the sixties, a decade that saw the rise of the modern world from the wreckage of World War II. It was the age of President John F. Kennedy, the first manned space flights, the Third World's green revolution in agriculture, the Civil Rights movement, and women's rights. The Council Fathers judged rightly that it was time for the Church to find a new language to speak the eternal truths of Faith to modern men and women. I remember the excitement when people heard the Church speaking in a way that was straightforward, biblical, personal, and pastoral."

And later on he wrote: "It is time for us to wake to the fact that during and after the Council, giants have walked among us: Blessed John XXIII, Blessed Mother Teresa, the Servants of God Paul VI and John Paul II, Cardinals de Lubac and Rahner, Fr von Balthasar, Br Roger of Taizé, Archbishop Romero, Dietrich von Hildebrand, Pope Benedict XVI, and many more." Among those he might have counted Marthe Robin, whose Foyers of Charity did so much to prepare for and fulfil Vatican II.

The Canonical Structures of the Foyers

The "Canonical Structures" of the Foyers, first submitted to and approved *ad experimentum* by Rome in 1986, and finally approved by Cardinal Stafford of the Pontifical Council for the Laity in 1999, throw useful light on the purpose and life of the Foyers. The first point to notice is that there is no single model of a Foyer. There is rather that marvellous diversity which the Lord accomplishes constantly in his Church, and which gives to each Foyer its separate character, within the unity of all, for the greater glory of the Church. The original Foyer at Châteauneuf remains the Central Foyer, to which the representatives of the 75 Foyers world-wide come every so often; but they must not be thought of as clones. While the spirit of the Foyers will be evident in all, there will be national and cultural differences.

When Fr Finet met Marthe for the first time in 1936, she told him how Jesus had prepared for that occasion mystically some years earlier. "It was then that Jesus spoke to me of the splendid work that He wanted to achieve here (in Châteauneuf) to the Glory of the Father, for the extension of His Reign in all the Church, and for the regeneration of the entire world, by means of the religious teaching that would be given here, the divine action of which would extend to the whole world. This was the Work to which I was to devote myself, following His commandments and His divine counsels. I would be under the direction of the priest whom from the beginning He had chosen and selected in His Heart for His edification, and to whom one day He would give faithful and devoted collaborators. They would help him to absolve, instruct, and nourish souls, and lead them to His Love."

" 'My most Holy Mother, who will be the Queen gloriously loved and listened to in this Foyer of My Love, which she will lead with her maternal presence, will achieve a veritable triumph within it. It will echo far and wide, and will be known in the remotest corners of the earth.'

"After that He spoke to me of the Work which would be a refuge for people in great human distress, who will come there to seek consolation and hope. 'Let it be the House of My Heart open to all. I want it to be a Foyer resplendent with Light, Charity, and Love.' "

The Foyers and the New Pentecost of Love

Marthe saw the Foyers as part of a "New Pentecost of Love" which would lead to the renewal of the Church, and the regeneration of the world. When she expressed concern that such a weak person as herself could collaborate in this work, so stupendously great, she was told: "Do not tremble; it is I who shall do everything." As we have seen, the first Foyer was founded by Fr Georges Finet in 1936, and grew during the Second World War. Others were gradually established, first in France and then in francophone places abroad, until by the time Marthe and Fr Finet were dead they were spreading all over the world. As already remarked, I have visited five in France, two in India, and one in the United States, and, though each has a character of its own, I was able to sense a strong common spirit.

As the text of the Canonical Structures puts it: "The reality of life in the Foyers goes beyond abstract definition. It is rooted in the invisible, in the Mystery of Christ, such as

Marthe lived it herself and called us to transform our lives and shine in our communities."

The Spirit is never weary of doing something new in the Church. The foundation of new ecclesial communities, as we see them today, should not surprise us. The definition of the Foyers, given by Fr Finet in 1971, remains the best summary of what the Foyers are, and seek to achieve.

"The Foyers of Charity are communities of baptised men and women who, following the example of the early Christians, share in common their material, intellectual and spiritual goods, and undertake to live together in the same spirit in order to bring about, with Mary as their Mother, the Family of God on earth, under the guidance of a priest, the Father, in a continuous effort of charity between themselves. By their life of prayer and work in the world they bear witness to Light, Charity and Love, according to the great message of Christ, King, Prophet and Priest."

Characteristics of the Foyers

Perhaps the most essential hallmark of the Foyers is their consecration to Mary, the Mother of the Church. Each of us is called, like St John, to take Mary into our home, and this is what every member of a Foyer tries to do. "My Holy Mother will be the Queen, gloriously loved and listened to, in this Foyer of my Love, which she will lead herself by her maternal presence," said Jesus to Marthe. (And after all, the word Foyer is synonymous with our word "home"). That is why the daily prayers in the Foyers include the words of consecration composed by St Louis de Montfort who also wrote: "It is through the most Blessed Virgin that Jesus Christ came into the world, and it is also by her that He must reign in the world." (*True Devotion*).

The next remarkable hallmark is the close association of laity and ordained priests. This was something which hardly existed in the pre-conciliar Church. One recalls the remark made in 1859 regarding the laity by Mgr George Talbot, in protesting against the more enlightened views of John Henry Newman: "What is the province of the laity? To hunt, to shoot, to entertain." They did indeed contribute substantially to the renewal of the Church in Victorian times, (cf. Madeleine Beard's *Faith and Fortune*, Gracewing), but physically and spiritually there was a fairly wide gulf fixed between clerics and laity until the mid-twentieth century.

For a priest to live in community with lay people was, in 1936, unusual if not unique. *Lumen Gentium*, perhaps the most important document to come out of Vatican II, redefined the link between the ordained priesthood and the laity, stressing that both are equally called to holiness (32). In this way a new emphasis was laid on the idea of family; on one side were the married families, on whom civilisation depended, and on the other families of lay persons around a priest, consecrating their lives to the service of God. For this reason the great majority of Foyer members are celibate, though in certain cases married families are closely linked to some Foyers.

The third unusual feature of the Foyers is that men and women live together in the same community. I can just remember a high Anglican church in Oxford where men sat on one side and women on the other, and this is still the practice in many churches in India. Before Vatican II it was almost unknown for men and women to go on retreat together, let alone live in community. Thus the first Foyer was entirely innovative. That this is now accepted without an eyebrow being raised shows the extent to which Vatican II has been influential in the Church, despite some resistance. Celibacy is possible in a mixed community though the pre-Conciliar Church did not believe this. "The communities of the Foyers unite lay persons and priests, men and women, people from various nations and cultures, in the service of the same mission to announce 'the Good News' to all."

Which brings us to the "mission" of the Foyers. Their apostolic work is principally to form and educate lay people through retreats. These, according to Our Lord's instructions to Marthe, were to last for five whole days and were to be experienced in silence. Thus, typically, retreatants arrive on a Sunday afternoon, listen to three conferences a day from the retreat conductor, pray Morning and Evening Prayer and the Holy Rosary daily, and of course attend a daily Mass. They do not chat among themselves, and music is played (over speakers) at meals. On Thursday night there is usually the chance to spend an hour or two keeping vigil with the Blessed Sacrament exposed. The retreat ends with the Montfortian consecration to Jesus through Mary, and the retreatants disperse on Saturday. There will be two talking meals, one at the beginning and one at the end. Members of the community not only see to the welfare of their visitors, but some will attend the retreat with them.

A Typical Foyer Retreat

The retreat which I and three other English people followed at Courset, a mere fifteen miles inland from Boulogne, and so very accessible to England, was typical of a retreat in any of the seventy plus Foyers, though obviously there will be local variations. On our arrival we were greeted with tea or coffee and shown to our comfortable purpose-built single or double rooms, each with its own wash place, WC and shower. At 6:30 we assembled in the chapel, the upper part of a cleverly converted stable-block of the mid-nineteenth century country house which forms the nucleus of the Foyer. After being greeted by Père Tierny who founded the Foyer in the seventies, the retreatants joined with the community in adoring the Blessed Sacrament and receiving Benediction. We then moved downstairs to a large covered area between house and stable known as "La Terrasse," where about 150 of the 200 school children were assembled sitting on the carpets, surrounded by thirty or forty chairs on which we sat. A touching ceremony followed in which Père Tierny got each visitor to introduce him or herself, after which an appointed child emerged from the throng who would become a sort of godchild for the week and form a prayer link with that grown-up. Mine was a charming nine year old called Benoit, whom I met on three occasions.

We then had our first meal, a wholesome four-course affair, taken in silence at round tables for eight, with classical music playing over the speakers. The food was beautifully cooked and served, and I noticed that special diets were sensitively catered for. Evening Prayer concluded the day, and we retired thankfully to our warm rooms.

Next morning began the routine which we were to follow for five days. We were wakened by music playing in the corridors at 7:30 and half-an-hour later we were at Morning Prayer in the chapel. This was conducted by "Le Père" with leisurely pace, commenting on each psalm and giving us thoughts for the day. The instrument which accompanied hymns and psalms was a zither, highly suitable for a fairly confined space. The altar is a massive oval piece of polished wood. A simple tabernacle is set against the wall behind it, with a Russian icon of Our Lady hanging nearby. Chairs extend in rows of seven the length of the chapel and a couple of rows are set along the right-hand side.

8:30 and the bell sounds for petit déjeuner: coffee or tea with the usual bread, butter and jam. At 9:15 we assemble in the conference room below the Chapel. Both are in strikingly good taste, like everything in the Foyer, their walls lined with coconut fibre. We sit at tables for four with bibles and note-books at the ready. First a brief practice of the chants for the day at Mass and Evening Prayer. Then Père Tierny arrives and begins with a "Réjouis-toi, Marie, comblée de grace..." a nice variation of the old "Je vous salue, Marie..." He then launches into an hour of brilliant commentary on the chosen theme, apparently without a note, illustrated with New Testament texts, filled with valuable insights, and spiced with personal reminiscences and digressions. This pattern is to be maintained for three sessions each day for five days. The solid

formation given by such rich fare is the hall-mark of all the
Foyers, as Marthe intended, but I cannot help feeling that the
conferences are at their very best at Courset. It was noticeable
how frequently Père Tierny quoted Marthe. Another he
mentioned several times was Cardinal Newman.

The daily Mass was at 11:15. Père Tierny concelebrated
with two other priests. At each of three of the Masses there
was a group of children from the school, and at the homily
time Père Tierny gave us a skilful demonstration of teaching
methods as he involved the children in the thought process
by means of question and answer. How well those youngsters
had been taught; and with what love and evident joy they
were lapping up the Faith; one felt they must surely already be
committed to the Lord's service for life. Marthe had shown
the value of children in the life of a Foyer: here was tangible
evidence of this fact. "Unless you be converted, and become
as little children, you shall not enter into the kingdom of
heaven," (Mt 18:3).

Lunch follows the Mass, and a strong "cidre bouché" is
drunk, the nectar of the north. Again lunch comprises four
courses, followed by coffee. Le Père tells the story of how in
the early days they economised by serving only three courses.
When the invalid, bedridden Marthe, with her usual cheerful
curiosity about every detail regarding her friends' lives asked
what the retreatants had to eat at Courset, le Père replied, "a
starter, a main dish, and a sweet." There was a pause, and
Marthe inquired "et le fromage?" Ever since, cheese has been
served at both meals!

After a break comes the afternoon talk, and then a
beautiful rosary conducted in "La Terrasse". This too involves
groups of the children who remain for one or two decades.
Another break is followed by a 'goûter' and at 5.45 the third
instruction. From this we return upstairs to the Chapel for an
hour's silent prayer before the exposed Blessed Sacrament.
Here we have a chance to continue savouring the graces of
our morning Communion, to share the presence of our

Blessed Lord with the other retreatants and community members, and to pray for the intentions which we and the children have written on pieces of paper and placed in the basket at the foot of the altar. What the French call "un temps fort" indeed.

Next comes supper—no cider or coffee—and we are free until Evening Prayer ends the day at 9:15. Here I should mention once again a detail found in some Foyers, namely a large basket marked "Corbeille de Marthe." In her lifetime, Marthe was most solicitous in sending help to those who were in real need, particularly prisoners and the young Foyers in developing countries. With her helpers she collected, packed and despatched innumerable parcels. This custom continues, and into Marthe's basket go packets of cigarettes, bars of chocolate, cakes of soap, Bibles, prayer books and rosaries, and other small gifts which are then parcelled and sent to prisons or poor Foyers.

Thus the five days succeeded one another all too quickly. On Monday there was an all-night vigil, and we took it in turns to pray for an hour before the Blessed Sacrament. The same happened after the New Year's Eve Midnight Mass. In those hours we tried, in Marthe's words, "to go beyond the threshold of our souls," to deepen our love of God, and to make it possible to return to the world better able to help our friends and neighbours in their quest for reality.

Foyer Schools and Organisation

The Courset Foyer has over two hundred children in its school, nearly forty members in the community, and it can accommodate as many as two hundred retreatants during holiday time or one hundred during term time. This evident renewal of the Church which was initiated just before World War II, when Marthe foresaw a "new Pentecost of Love," is no small-scale affair.

A subsidiary work is to welcome "the many distressed people who will come to seek consolation and hope and the shelter of its walls ... I want it (the Foyer) to be a life-giving oasis for souls of goodwill, for souls who are anxious and discouraged, to hardened and sceptical sinners: the House of my Heart, open to everyone!"

Apart from Courset, a number of Foyers run schools, notably Châteauneuf and Vellore in India, which require a fair proportion of their members to be involved with the care and education of their pupils. The Central Foyer at Châteauneuf, which started in 1934 as a school for local girls of primary age, now has 400 girls of all ages, many of whom board, and there are some 400 boys in a separate school at Saint-Bonnet. These schools have been a striking source of vocations to the priesthood and the religious life in France, as well as to the Foyers.

"The Foyers continue the assembly and the mission of the Apostolic Community in the Church for the glory of Christ, Saviour of the world."

They take as their model the Pentecostal Community described by St Luke in the first chapter of Acts. There is quite a strong charismatic element in a number of the communities, as well as Marian, Eucharistic and Papal facets. It is interesting that it is the bishops of the growing Church in the developing world, e.g., in Africa, who are extremely keen to welcome a Foyer into their dioceses. They are thus part of the evangelisation movement that St Thérèse was so keen to foster, and they reflect the "New Pentecost of Love" forecast by Marthe. Prayer lies at the heart of every community, and finds its centre and summit in the daily Eucharist.

The financial support for the communities comes mainly from the (voluntary) donations of the retreatants. Like independent schools, Foyers rely on occasional appeals for building and expansion; also for the support of Third World Foyers. Occasionally Foyer members take paid jobs outside, but by and large there is enough work within the Foyer to keep everyone occupied. The expansion of the Foyers I have visited has been remarkable, and was especially striking at the two in India, which have been greatly helped from France. The other notable feature of Foyer communities is the climate of joyfulness; they know how to celebrate feasts as well as how to fast.

All this requires and presupposes organisation. There is a well-devised structure that backs up the life of each Foyer. The day-to-day running of a Foyer is in the hands of a council of lay members led by what the French call *le responsable*. He or she is a lay person. The priest (also on the council) is responsible for the spiritual life of the Foyer, and preaches the retreats; but he is not the superior "in charge". His role is that of a father, rather than director. "He lives his priesthood in the heart of the community in order that all may fulfil their vocation to live the priesthood of the laity." There may be more than one priest in any Foyer. A candidate seeking to join a community serves a period of three years before being invited to make a commitment as a full and permanent member. This is rather like final vows in a religious order; but Foyer members do not take vows, nor do they wear a habit or uniform. "Despite all our imperfections, it must be possible to say of us as of the first Christians: 'See how they love one another'. Tertullian adds: 'The world would not have believed if they had not loved one another so much.' This remains true today."

Not only are there the fundamental retreats aimed at instructing and inspiring ordinary lay people; there are also specialist retreats on particular themes that are addressed to various groups such as priests, nuns, catechists, engaged or married couples, young people, and so on. Short weekends are arranged for busy working people who may not be able to get away for a whole week. "Many people are living in the dark. They no longer know the meaning of life, nor the meaning of history, because they no longer know Christ the Light of the World." And just as so many of the early retreatants under Fr Finet at Châteauneuf met and came to know Marthe, so latter day ones encounter her still. She is very much spiritually present at every retreat.

The Diocese and the Church

Every Foyer is a cell within the Church. Like Marthe, they are always conscious of belonging to the universal Church. In particular they have a deep and filial relationship with their bishops. A new Foyer can only start at the request or consent of a local bishop. "The faithful must adhere to the Bishop, just as the Church adheres to Jesus Christ, and Jesus Christ to the Father" (*Lumen Gentium* 27). Thus the relations between the fathers and the lay members of a Foyer and their Bishop are firmly based on the teaching of Vatican II. They are part of the universal mission of the Church for the regeneration of the whole world.

Thus the vision of the Foyer Movement is universal, and already we can see how Foyers have been established in many parts of the world. This very universalism implies diversity; there is no single model of a Foyer, though all are closely linked to Châteauneuf, the central Foyer. "This wonderful diversity, taken over and purified by the Gospel, achieves in its harmony the fullness of man in Christ, to the Glory of the Father." So the mother-house remains a centre of unity, to which Foyer Fathers and members come regularly from all over the world, especially now that international air travel has become so easy. It resembles the centre of a huge extended family, and is filled with the memory and the spirit of Marthe Robin. We remember, too, the saying of Père Michon: "The Foyers have only just begun."

Only the power of the Risen Christ is able to transform the world. We rely in faith on this Word which still says to us: "I am with you all days, even to the consummation of the world," (Mt 28:20), and, "have confidence, I have overcome the world," (Jn 16:33).

11

The Divine Mercy, the
Eucharist, and the Church

When Marthe was three years old, a girl was born to a humble family in Poland and was christened Helena Kowalska, taking the name Faustina in religious life. She, like Marthe, was destined by God to play an important role in the life of the Church of the twentieth and twenty-first Centuries. Can any connection be established between these two women?

On the face of it very little. But I think the spiritual influence of these two mystics can be linked and contrasted. They were virtually the same age, and it was in the middle twenties that both received their vocations, albeit very different ones. Marthe's was to become increasingly handicapped and to share mystically in Our Lord's Passion. Faustina's was to receive a call to the religious life, in which she joined an order called the Sisters of Our Lady of Mercy. She joined that order in 1925 at the age of nineteen, against her family's wishes. Like Marthe she was one of a large family whose father was a small peasant farmer, and neither of them received much formal elementary education.

St Faustina kept a diary of her experiences and reflections, under the instructions of her eventual confessor and spiritual director, Blessed Fr Sopocko. This diary, now seen as a document of Catholic mysticism of exceptional worth, was only publicised in 1979, after the Vatican had withdrawn its reservations on the Divine Mercy devotion, and was translated into English with the help of a number of different people in the early eighties, shortly after Marthe's death. She herself left a large quantity of writing, most of it dictated, much of which is still unpublished. Both Marthe's writing and St Faustina's have the same quality, that of being exceptionally profound yet expressed in simple language, one in French and the other in Polish. The challenge of translating these texts has been likened to that facing the translators of Sacred Scripture. The other thing both these mystics have in common is that they were chosen by God to receive private revelations and messages. These of course are subject to examination and authentication by the Church.

The Divine Mercy apostolate had been delayed nearly twenty years (1959-78) due to faulty information being given to the Holy See, and it was only in 1978, when the Cardinal Archbishop of Krakow, Karol Wojtyla, was elected Pope, that these reservations were withdrawn. He had already initiated her beatification process in 1965, and this reached its conclusion in Rome in 1993. Seven years later St Faustina was the first saint to be proclaimed in the New Millennium.

St Faustina's Mission

She began writing her diary in 1934, in a series of notebooks, at the same time describing her life in the order from 1925. From her earliest days in the convent she had received locutions from heaven, but none but her superiors and confessors were aware of this. Like Marthe, she kept hidden her mystical experiences as far as she could. At the end of her first year in the noviciate she suffered the spiritual trial known, (from St John of the Cross), as the "dark night of the soul." After a while, she turned to St Thérèse, who earlier had been one of her heroines, and in a dream she received a visit from the "Little Flower" who encouraged her to persevere and accept whatever suffering God might send her. In the diary she describes how Thérèse told her that one day she too would be a saint raised to the altars.

As we have seen, this is a significant link with Marthe, who at almost the same time (1926) had three "visits" from St Thérèse, when she was very ill, who told her she would not die but would carry on her work of evangelisation. In April 1928, Sr Faustina and a few companions made their vows of simple profession for one year, but her dark night continued. However, that October, Mother Michael, who had admitted Faustina to the order, was elected Superior General, and she was to become her chief source of support and consolation.

St Faustina had much suffering in her brief few years in the various convents to which she was assigned, both physical and spiritual. Neither her superiors nor her confessors were able to help her on several occasions, as they failed to recognise the advanced spiritual experiences Our Lord was sending her. Some of her fellow sisters even regarded her as slightly mad. Just as Marthe prayed specially for France, so Faustina prayed for Poland. She saw in prophecy the coming turmoil, and in particular the suffering of Warsaw. Nonetheless, she believed her country would be much blessed. It was in the 1930's that St Faustina received the detailed instructions from Jesus regarding the image of himself to be painted, the Divine Mercy chaplet to be said on rosary beads, and the request for a feast day to be celebrated on Low Sunday.

It was in these same years that Marthe was receiving detailed instructions regarding the foundation of the school at Châteauneuf, and after the providential meeting with Father Finet in 1936, the foundation of the first Foyer of Charity. St Faustina died of tuberculosis—like St Thérèse—in 1938, after much suffering, and the following year the Nazis invaded Poland, starting World War II. At the same time the first Foyer was being built, while the German army was occupying a good part of France.

The Divine Mercy

In April 1933, Sr Faustina and two others returned to Krakow for a retreat before taking final vows. On the fourth day she went to see another of her confessors, Fr Andrasz, and told him of Jesus' request for a picture to be painted of Divine Mercy. Father's recommendation was that she should find a permanent spiritual director. It was the Jubilee Year of the Lord's Passion. She was then posted to Vilnius in Lithuania, where she worked in the garden, and there she remained for three years. On the way she visited Czestochowa for the first time. At Vilnius she was welcomed by the other sisters, and there at last she found her permanent director, Fr Michael Sopocko, now beatified. He accepted the reality of the visions and messages which she told him about, and in 1934 he commissioned a local artist to make the first Divine Mercy picture, following Sr Faustina's instructions. It was then that Jesus told Sr Faustina the meaning of the red and white rays issuing from his Heart, that is that they represented blood and water, the life and cleansing of souls. At Vilnius she began to suffer seriously, both physically and spiritually, and on Holy Thursday 1934 she made an Act of Oblation, offering herself for the conversion of sinners. Jesus accepted it with the words "I am giving you a share of the Redemption of mankind." It was then that He requested that the first Sunday after Easter be celebrated as the Feast of Mercy.

Later that year it was Christ's mother who came to warn her that she was to be tested by illness. She was also assailed by demons, which appeared to her like a pack of black dogs. In August she collapsed, and was given the Sacrament of the Sick by Fr Sopocko. All this was very similar to the experiences of Marthe Robin in the twenties and thirties: she too had a mystical relationship with Jesus and Mary, and she too suffered frequent diabolical attacks. She also expected to die young. And both shared the sufferings of the Passion, but in different ways. The incredible value of prayer was revealed to both. But whereas Faustina received her Lord daily in the Eucharist, Marthe did so only once a week, and never attended the Holy Sacrifice of the Mass.

Marthe and the Eucharist

Despite this, it is none the less true to say that her life was centred around the Eucharist, and Fr Raymond Peyret described it in the title of his third book as: "The Long Mass of Marthe Robin."

At the Colloquium held at Châteauneuf on the 6th and 7th June 2003, Fr Maurice Gardes was invited to speak on Marthe as "A Eucharistic Mystic." He told how he first met Marthe as a seminarian on retreat, and then again as a young priest in 1975, some years before her death. The Church was in a state of turmoil at the time, and he asked her what she thought about a certain current dispute. Her response was immediate: "What does your bishop think?" He uses this story to illustrate that Marthe was first and foremost a daughter of the Church; and he also quotes Jean Guitton, whom he met in Paris, who said of her: "A genius ... the greatest genius I have ever met." "How would you define genius, Maitre?" to which he replied: "Someone who associates the sublime with the banality of everyday life."

Fr Maurice goes on to quote from Marthe's Journal of 1930 to 1932, with comments of his own.

"O Saviour Jesus! Before you died you gave us—through a prodigy of love—your flesh to eat and your blood to drink, so that we might have your life in us." (18 April 1930)

"O God! You my Lord, most loving of all hearts, believe in my love. Holy Communion—sweet banquet for my soul. Each time it is renewed, it produces in me a more perfect happiness, and a greater love for the Holy Eucharist." (2 March 1931)

"Holy Communion ... My soul thirsts for the God of Love! Yesterday I was overwhelmed with suffering, beneath the

Cross, plunged into bitterness, weighed down by my burdens. Then Jesus came to me in such manifest love, and my soul was embalmed by such great tenderness. Jesus comes and lives in me, and my soul is made peaceful, consoled and happy." (12 April 1930)

But three days later ... "My God, my God, why have you abandoned me? In my poor little soul there is a dark night, without a single star shining. Jesus remains deaf to my desperate appeals ... in the cold gloom where my soul dwells, the mockings of the devil ceaselessly incite me to despair ... nothing can compare with this trial of the soul attacked by its spiritual enemy when its defender leaves it alone during the night. Yet I cling to the arms of my Jesus, abandoning myself to his power, recalling the words He once said to me: 'You are nothing, but I am everything.' I know that God's goodness cannot deceive our hearts." (15 April 1930)

More than once Marthe refers to what she sees as "diabolical temptations" to despair, such as other saints have experienced. Her life was an extraordinary combination of the Cross and the Joy. In February 1930, she quoted from St Catherine of Siena in a similar situation, ending with:

"We must therefore always and in spite of everything cling to the conviction that God is not unconcerned when we suffer, that He is with us in our pain even more than in our happiness, and that He counts all the drops of sweat that fall from our foreheads, and all the tears we shed for love of Him." (27 February 1930)

"I have no other dream than to conform myself at every moment with the suffering and Eucharistic life of our Divine Saviour, to unite my host with His Host, so that my heart may be consecrated with His Heart to the Glory of the Father for the salvation of the world. For the more my life is submitted to God and in conformity with the Redeemer, the more I shall participate in the achievement of His Work." (11 August 1932)

And Fr Maurice concludes: "May the experience of Jesus' disciples, of Marthe, and of so many Christians, give us the taste for the Eucharist! By receiving and eating the bread of immortality, we consume the fire of the Holy Spirit that will make us into prophets, of which our world has such need."

Marthe – Daughter of the Church

Monsignor Didier Marchand, the Bishop of Valence at the time of her death, read a paper on the theme of Marthe as a daughter of the Church at the Colloquium of 2003.

He said that she was a daughter of the Church because she was first a daughter of God. She was totally abandoned to the Saviour. He quoted from her Acts of Abandonment of 1925 and 1926; also from her journal in 1930: "All perfection is in love ... all holiness is in humility." He notes that essentially it was in her sharing in the Passion of Christ that she derived her strength, and found her true place in the Church. For it was at Calvary that the Church was born.

She was also a true daughter of the Church in her submission to the guidance, first of Fr Faure and then of Fr Finet. She practised what Vatican II was to teach about the role of the laity in *Lumen Gentium*: "The vocation of lay people is to search for the reign of God over temporal affairs ... the laity is called by God to work for the sanctification of the world." (31) The opening of the school in 1934 and the founding of the first Foyer in 1936 were both missionary works of the Church. And every Foyer throughout the world is linked with a bishop of a diocese. These Foyers of light, charity and love are communities in the spirit of Vatican II, linking lay people and priests in the service of evangelisation.

Marthe showed herself to be a daughter of the Church in her high regard for the priesthood, and in her constant desire to help priests. She made a point of insisting that Priests on Foyer retreats be "well looked-after" (*bien soignés*). At the same time she approved of the Council's insistence on the priesthood of all the baptised members of the Church. She herself lived that priesthood. "The common priesthood of the faithful and the ministerial priesthood are closely linked, even though there is an essential difference between them ... both participate in the unique priesthood of Christ," (*Lumen Gentium* 10).

Here is one of her prayers for priests. "O Lord, renew your first Pentecost. Dear Jesus, give to all your beloved priests the grace of the discerning of spirits; fill them with your gifts; increase their love; make valiant apostles of them all, and real saints among men," (25 May 1939).

When Marthe died, Mgr Marchand heard from more than fifty priests or seminarians who testified to the influence Marthe had had in their lives. Another proof that she was a true daughter of the Church was the number of bishops and cardinals who visited her at La Plaine. She had, too, an immense respect for the several popes who reigned during her lifetime, all of whom, from Pius XII onwards, were aware of her.

Another piece of evidence quoted by Bishop Marchand is Marthe's remark to Fr Finet at their famous first encounter: "Yes, you must remain under obedience (to your religious superiors)." She herself never suggested any initiative without first referring it to her bishop. Today all the Foyers are present in all sorts of dioceses at the invitation of the bishop.

Marthe and the Foyers are inseparable. Announcing a new Pentecost of Love, she showed her deep attachment to the Church. She visualised the Apostles surrounding the Mother of God, as reported by St Luke in Acts. When John Paul II was elected to the Papacy in 1978, she remarked: "This Pope is chosen by the Blessed Virgin." In the Body of Christ we must all be sons and daughters of the Church, but Marthe was this par excellence.

Mgr Marchand concludes his intervention with this passage:

"Instead of giving way to her handicap, she transfigures it by giving herself to the Saviour.

Instead of remaining in a routine of pious practice, she places herself unreservedly in His hands.

Instead of remaining immobile on her bed, she founds Foyers of light, charity and love throughout the world.

Instead of remaining inactive, she plays her part as a committed lay woman.

Instead of regarding herself as someone important, she knows how small she is, and relies on God's mercy.

Instead of complaining, she makes of her suffering something great and fruitful.

Instead of regretting her state of life, she transforms it into a paschal joy.

Instead of relying on herself, she acts and holds her place as a Daughter of the Church."

Right at the end of the Colloquium, Mgr Marchand closed the proceedings with further words of wisdom, throwing more light on the nature of this extraordinary woman. It was the first of its kind, and he hopes there may be others in due course. He also hopes there may be further books written on Marthe, thereby encouraging the author of this short study. He says Marthe needs to be better known. She is important for the Church today, which has evolved and is evolving rapidly in a changing world.

And the Foyers have an important part to play in this evolution. Marthe both anticipated and fulfilled the intuitions of Vatican II; and as she said: "she carries us in her prayer."

12

Thoughts from Père Ravanel

Père Jacques Ravanel was close to Fr Finet for nearly forty years. In 2008, he published a book on Marthe called *Le Secret de Marthe Robin*. Half a century earlier he had founded the Foyer set in a spectacular situation in the Alps named "La Flatière". When Fr Finet died in 1991, he was chosen to become his successor at Châteauneuf, and it was he who was the first Postulator of Marthe's cause. He now gives us his *memoires* of Marthe, based on the many texts left to us, first by the Abbé Faure, and then by her several secretaries who recorded Marthe's sayings and reflections over the years. As Mgr Marchand, Bishop of Valence in Marthe's last years and writer of the preface to Fr Ravanel's book says: "This book deserves more than a simple reading; it invites us to a veritable meditation." In this chapter I shall try and summarise some of his insights.

He sees Marthe essentially as a contemplative. In her youth she found God in the beauty of nature. As she grew up and became more and more handicapped, she came to resemble her Saviour and to share his joys and sufferings. By totally abandoning herself to his will she reached the very summits of contemplation and, like St Thérèse, became identified with love. She no longer lived, but Christ lived in her. Yet to all appearances she remained an ordinary country woman who met, talked with, and influenced, many thousands of visitors over fifty years.

Marthe's Notebooks

When Marthe died in 1981, Fr Finet discovered in her room a collection of notebooks in which Abbé Faure had written down her thoughts and sayings between 1929 and 1932. These were later passed into the care of Fr Ravanel, and he has made good use of them to examine Marthe's spiritual growth. It was indeed a time rich in supernatural graces, preparing her for her great mission, including the stigmata. What struck him particularly were the expressions of joy mingled with accounts of her suffering. Père Raymond Peyret certainly found the ideal title for his first biography: *The Cross and the Joy.*

Fr Ravanel traces the comparative normality of her childhood up to the age of sixteen, with her lifelong sense of humour and fun. He recalls the anecdote of how she pinned a rabbit's tail on to the back of a man's jacket at the village fair, and how she loved to laugh at amusing stories. He quotes a neighbour who wrote later about how Marthe delighted in the array of flowers in the garden at La Plaine. He notes that the family were not regular Catholics but "occasional conformists" who went to Mass on the major feasts. The Robins got on well with their neighbours the Achards, and in the winter they shared long fireside evenings, talking of the recent war, the crops and the livestock, and playing card games. Max Achard recalls that Marthe was always full of gaiety, and how they all laughed a great deal.

Catechism was taught to children in a fairly dry way in those days, and Fr Ravanel quotes another Foyer Father who remembers Marthe saying to him: "No doubt when you were a child people spoke to you about God, as they did to me. And then I opened the Gospels and found He was the Father!" It was the mind rather than the heart that was addressed in religious teaching, and the word love was rarely mentioned.

But at least children were introduced to prayer, and Marthe
famously remarked later: "As a young girl I always loved *Le
Bon Dieu.*" Fr Ravanel emphasises once again the impact
made on her by her first Communion in 1912. He also notes
how her mother never turned away a beggar from her door but
always gave him something to eat.

He quotes from Fr Finet's notes of 1943, when Marthe
reminisced about her youth, and how she loved to pray,
especially to Our Lady, and how she went regularly to
confession. She found God both in nature and in her fellows,
and particularly in priests—the sight of a priest always moved
her. On one occasion she went to some woods to look for wild
strawberries for her mother, and inadvertently trod on an
adder which failed to bite her but pursued her, after which she
had a horror of snakes. She was very close to both her parents,
especially her father. She found her brother Henri shy and
gauche. And she told Fr Finet how much she missed her
eldest sister Célina when she married M. Serve, with whom
she never really hit it off.

Marthe's Illness

Everything was to change in 1918, with the onset of constant
illness. Her contemplative nature was to grow into an
extraordinary sanctity. Paraphrasing the Roman saying about
a healthy mind in a healthy body, Marthe said: "A healthy
mind in a sick body is even more beautiful." She grew to
accept her pain and limitations with love, and to become
more and more identified with her Saviour. In 1930 she
wrote: "Pain and suffering do not come from heaven, but help
to bear them does, leading to happiness." Fr Ravanel draws
principally on the evidence produced in 1942 by the two
doctors who examined her at the request of Fr Finet, and also
on the reports of Dr Assailly, and he summarises her medical
condition year by year from 1918 to 1929.

In 1922, quoting Dr Assailly, he says that Marthe borrowed
a book from the parish library about a Visitation nun who

died in 1916 and who claimed that Our Lord had said to her mystically: "I am preparing my work of mercy. I want a fresh resurrection in society, and it must be the work of love on which I place no limits. You can give me souls by your sacrifice. The world is heading for a precipice. I shall prevent it from going over the edge by means of a small battalion of generous souls who will fight under my leadership." It was that same year that Marthe came across the book in an old trunk in her sister's attic in which she read: "You ask for rest ... but you must prepare for suffering." With hindsight we can see it as a strange prophecy. It was then, too, that she began to wear glasses for reading and embroidery.

Another Crisis

In October 1927, she went through another medical crisis and received the last sacraments for the third time. She could do nothing without the help of her mother, whose own health was none too good. She wrote around this time: "I am experiencing how sweet it is to love, even when suffering. Suffering is the incomparable school of real love." And meditating on the incredible suffering of Christ she wrote: "Every drop of Christ's blood speaks a language of eternity." And later: "With what love Jesus surrounds my suffering life!" "It seems to me that Jesus is imprinting very strongly in me the Love of the intimate dolours of his most Holy Mother and of his Redeeming Passion." She was indeed being prepared for the great sharing of his Passion that was to come in the thirties.

Early in 1929 paralysis seized both her legs and arms, and she was no longer able to leave her couch or embroider. Her inability to eat or drink normally began now; she suffered frequent headaches and had few visitors. Her long struggle to overcome her handicaps was over, and she was now totally dependent on her family and on God.

So we come to 1930 when Our Blessed Lord united himself to Marthe in a special way, and she began her weekly experiences of his Passion, Death and Resurrection, which were to last nearly fifty years.

The Stigmata and the Passion

Fr Ravanel draws on the notes made by both Fr Faure and Fr Finet on Marthe's mystical phenomena. Again and again he finds references to the divine joy and graces that Marthe received from the love of God, which almost obliterate her sufferings. These notebooks (*cahiers*), and also her *Journal Intime*, are of the greatest value, and some have been published. They provide an extraordinary insight into the mystic's spiritual union with Jesus.

Fr Ravanel says that Marthe's comments often resemble the poems of St John of the Cross. "In her own way she recalls to us the presence of Jesus manifesting his love to the world, despite the violence of his adversaries. By the Cross, the Love of God remains rooted on this earth." In *Cahier* 22, written at the end of January 1945, Marthe gave Fr Finet a detailed and harrowing account of her experiencing the Flagellation, Crowning with Thorns, and Crucifixion. There is no indication of the Resurrection at this point, but we know she experienced this too. It is open for us too, says Fr Ravanel, to share with Marthe in this mystery.

As an authentic mystic she had complete confidence in the Church, and entrusted all her reflections to the discernment of her spiritual father. There is no doubt that her faith and her prayer acted as a constraint on the breakdown of her personality which the consequences of her illness might otherwise have caused. She sometimes linked her experiences with those of Blessed Anne-Catherine Emmerich, the German mystic, as interpreted by her amanuensis Clemens Brentano. Fr Ravanel quotes Cardinal Ratzinger in his commentary on Sr Lucia's account of the third part of secret of Fatima, to explain the significance of private revelations. Thus Marthe's visions are religious expressions whose origin lies in the mystery of God, but which depend on the human and psychological limits of their author. They must never amplify the simplicity of the Gospel descriptions.

Marthe was fully aware of the paradox of love and suffering that we find in the Passion of Jesus, and which can be seen in some of the Beatitudes. At the same time she constantly linked the sufferings of Jesus with those of his Mother, who shared completely with him the thirst to do the Father's will, in order to save countless souls out of love. Mary stood at the foot of the Cross with the Beloved Disciple, and is regarded as the Co-Redemptrix by the Church. She was with the incarnate Son of God at every crucial stage of his life on earth, which is why the Church exalts her above every creature and calls her Queen of Heaven.

The Divine Mercy

As Fr Ravanel points out, the Church in France as recently as Marthe's time was still influenced by the Jansenist heresy, which overstressed the demands of divine justice in the face of human sin. Marthe never followed this excess, any more than St Thérèse, and was much closer to the thought of her contemporary St Faustina in Poland. Divine mercy always overcame divine vengeance. God was always supremely a God of love; Fr Ravanel quotes Bossuet, the famous French Bishop, theologian, and orator to this effect; he flourished not long after Jansen was preaching in the seventeenth century. Thus, he says, Marthe lived the Passion of Jesus in a theological synthesis that depended on Him who was wholly love; his divine suffering became the expression of that love, which was not a necessary evil that justified sinful humans. Marthe's sufferings were a heart to heart with her Blessed Lord. "Jesus drew me lovingly into his arms; He spoke these words softly: 'No one apart from me, and my Mother, has ever suffered what you are suffering. I want you to share in all my sufferings, for the remission of all the sins of the world, and for all the people on earth ... you will be, with my most Holy

Mother, the Mediatrix and Co-Redemptrix of sinners.' "
(*Cahier* 10) This is surely quite extraordinary.

Marthe and the devil

Fr Ravanel gives several examples of diabolical attacks,
notably from Fr Finet's account of a Passion on the afternoon
of Friday 3 January 1941: "The demon threw her against the
chest of drawers (commode) and seemed to throttle her.
14:25. 'Go away! Oh go away!' 14:32. 'My God, my Father...'
—sound of throttling—she prays. 14:35. 'Yes Father,' pause;
she prays—agitation—another attack."

He comments how today many Catholics no longer
believe in the existence of the devil; and he quotes John Paul
II in his Apostolic Exhortation of 1986: "The Church
participates in the victory of Christ over the devil, for Christ
gave his disciples the power to drive out demons ..." And from
Gaudium et Spes: "By shedding his blood the innocent Lamb
has won us life, reconciling us with Himself and one another,
delivering us from the slavery to the devil." Thus, like Our
Lord, Marthe was assailed by the fallen angel Lucifer. And in
a reference to the *Catechism*, in the section on the *Pater
Noster*, he says: "the request to 'deliver us from evil' is not an
abstraction, but denotes a person—Satan, the evil one, the
angel opposed to God..." And we recall that there are any
number of references to Satan in the New Testament.

Fr Ravanel remarks on the three forms that diabolical
activity usually takes—possession, infestation, and
temptation. The first is rare and requires a trained exorcist to
deal with it. The second is seen in the lives of many saints,
like the Curé d'Ars, Padre Pio, Faustina, and Catherine
Emmerich. The third is the most common, experienced by all
of us. Clearly Marthe was afflicted by the second category,
infestation. Because she lived in the closest possible
relationship with Christ, Satan regularly and actively
attacked her, and as I have noted elsewhere only recourse to
the protection of Our Lady could be her defence. Even Fr

Finet found the situation impossible on occasions. In 1947, Marthe observed: "Sometimes his attacks are quite interior. He tries to convince me of the uselessness of my life and sufferings, hoping to discourage me and lead me to despair ... he attacks the Church, the Sovereign Pontiff, and priests."

In Blessed Mother Teresa's recently published private papers we can detect the same theme. In both her and in Marthe we can see evidence of "the dark night of the soul", and in both it is love that triumphs over discouragement. Just as Jesus never stopped praying to his Father throughout the Passion, so Marthe "wrote" in *Cahier* 11: "We must pray without ceasing as He did. His interior life was one big ecstasy ... what He wants above all for his disciples is the greatest of all gifts—intimate union with God— 'I in them, and you in Me', so that they may experience unity." (cf. Jn 17). This was Marthe's achievement, which she passes on to us.

A Foyer of Saints

Fr Ravanel recounts movingly how, in 1941, Marthe became convinced that Fr Finet (who had been ill, and absent for a while) was no longer interested in her or the Foyer, and that the work of the Foyer was over. She even wanted to destroy the document, which only saw the light of day in 1960, in which she had recorded the words of Jesus to her a decade earlier: "I want to do something new here, something very great for Our Glory, on account of all that I wish to do in and through you. I want to receive here infinite Love and Glory ... I want all the members of this work (*oeuvre*) to be saints! They must shine by the example of a profoundly supernatural life ... by giving themselves to each other, and in a total gift to God. I shall spread floods of light and grace on each member! ... My most Holy Mother will accomplish astonishing marvels here; marvels such as were seen in the Early Church will be repeated here.

"My most Holy Mother, who will be the Queen gloriously loved and listened to in the Foyer of my Love, will know a veritable triumph that will be celebrated in the most remote places on earth.

"The priest whom I am preparing to help you establish and develop this Foyer will be most influential ... he will not be able to do anything without you ... it is by you that I wish to transmit my orders, and to communicate to him my light and my grace. And you will be unable to do anything without him. I want to establish between you a perfect and intimate union, conceived in my Heart, a union like that between me and my most Holy Mother. The very angels will be moved by it. I have a mission to entrust to you, for the many souls that I wish to give you, for the Glory of my Name.

"Do not tremble ... it is I who will do everything. I shall be your light and strength. I shall be Love and Light in the life of each of the souls in whom I want to reign as Sovereign Master. The work will be a refuge for many in great human distress, who will come seeking comfort and hope ... innumerable sinners will come, drawn by my Mother and myself, in search of light and healing of their ills.

"I want it to be a Foyer filled with Light, Love and Charity, a special centre for spiritual resurrections ... the House of my Heart open to all."

13

Marthe's Life: A Summing Up

There is little question but that Marthe Robin was among the most outstanding characters of the twentieth century. But because of the obscurity of her life she is not easy to summarise or to place in relation to the events of that century. She undoubtedly left a deep impression on the many thousands of visitors that she received and talked with in her little room over a period of fifty years. But even they found her difficult to really understand. "She had the art of making us forget that she was even ill." "We were in the presence of someone who was living in our times," are two typical comments. Her human "normality" was what struck people, rather than her mystical "abnormality". "Living in the confines of a room of 12 square metres, she seemed nevertheless to be plunged into the heart of the world" was how Fr Ravanel described her in his reminiscences. "Marthe lived in the intimacy of Christ" was his own summing up.

Undoubtedly her private "writings" of the period 1929 to 1932 will in due course be more publicised, and will be studied by modern theologians; and when she is beatified a lot more attention will be focused on her. Meanwhile the great work of the Foyers of Charity—seventy-five worldwide—is making her known to the most disparate peoples of every race. It is my hope that this book will make her better known in the Anglophone world, which is constantly on the increase.

Here is a quotation from Marthe's "Intimate journal" dated 7 February 1932: "One has to live in the love of God, and to be reduced to inactivity by illness; I have to experience deeply this abasement, this weakness, and this poverty. 'Without Me you cannot be.' 'I am He who is.' Jesus affirms that, 'You have nothing but what you receive from Me.' He has given me extraordinary graces, and the greatest of all are the deep abysses He has dug within me. I need nothing but Him to fill my being and extend my soul." In a world consumed with the desire for material prosperity, these are sobering words. Fr Ravanel reflects that just as she helped more than a hundred thousand people to a more intimate union with God in her lifetime, so she continues to do so with countless admirers who turn to her in prayer today.

There is no doubt that Marthe carried on the work of the Little Flower (as she was told she would in 1926). The influence of St Thérèse in her lifetime was limited to her small community and the few seminarians and missionaries she was allowed to correspond with; whereas that of Marthe was extended to well over a hundred thousand men and women and, through the Foyers, to many others all over the world. Both were powerful apostles of God.

Marthe and Suffering

"Mary in Fatima came to evangelise our century," wrote Fr Cervera OCD in his preface to Sr Lucia's last book *Calls from the Message of Fatima* (1997). And one of the greatest evangelists of that century was the little handicapped country woman, bearer of Our Lord's stigmata, Marthe Robin. It seems that one day Marthe may be known as the "Patron of the Disabled." Perhaps the greatest message that can be derived from her astonishing life is that suffering can have a unique and powerful place in the life of the Church and its members. "Of all the forms of the apostolate, that of good works, that of prayer, that of example, that of suffering, this last apostolate is worth the most ..." In a world where, despite the best efforts of the secular humanists, there is still so much suffering, this message is very valuable. "My suffering is bathed in the joy of my loving; for it is joyful since it comes from love, and since it is redemptive for souls. How infinitely sweet is the thought that, as a member of the Body of Christ, all my pain and suffering, united to His loving suffering, share in its divine work." As Fr Michel Tierny says in his valuable short study of Marthe—reproduced in the CTS Booklet, *Marthe Robin: A Chosen Soul,* (B652)—"Her constant preoccupation was to bring to Jesus those who came to her." And this still happens in every Foyer.

What C. S. Lewis called the "Problem of Pain", the problem of why a loving God has created human beings in his image, who then often have to go through so much suffering during their lives, remains one of the chief reasons why so many cease to believe in a benevolent Creator. In recent times, Leonard Cheshire, founder of a large number of homes for the disabled all over the world, grappled with this problem in his final book, *Where is God in All This?* (St Paul Publications, 1991). The theological explanation is to be found in the early chapters of Genesis, and is known as the Fall, but many remain unconvinced by this.

It is my belief that the life and witness of Marthe Robin may shed light on this mystery, without of course solving it. The whole Christian religion is based on the life, death and Resurrection of Jesus Christ some two thousand years ago, and all His followers since have had to share that experience, to a greater or lesser degree. Marthe was among those who shared it to a very high degree; some would say a unique degree. And the fruit of her suffering with Christ is the large number of Foyers of Charity which attract so many members and retreatants in every part of the world. She was typically reticent about talking of her mystical experiences, but now, thirty years after her death, her friends are beginning to analyse and make sense of them.

We say of people like Marthe that she was a mystic. What does that mean? The Oxford Dictionary defines a mystic as: "A person who seeks by contemplation and self-surrender to obtain unity or identity with or absorption into the Deity or the ultimate reality, or who believes in the spiritual apprehension of truths that are beyond the understanding."

G.K. Chesterton wrote in 1901—as quoted by William Oddie in *Chesterton and the Romance of Orthodoxy*—"It is remarkable to notice even in daily life how constant is this impression of the essential rationality of mysticism ... Mysticism, in a sense of the mystery of things, is simply the most gigantic form of common-sense. We should not have to complain of any materialism if common-sense were only common." As so often, that great thinker hit the nail on the head with a neat paradox.

And so we must leave Marthe, and pray, like so many of her visitors, that she may sustain us through her intercession.

Bibliography

Antier, Jean-Jacques, *Marthe Robin, le Voyage Immobile,* (Perrin, 1990).

Assailly, Dr Alain, *Marthe Robin, Témoignage d'un Psychiatre,* (Emmanuel, 1996).

Escoulen, Daniel, *Si le Grain de Blé ne Meurt,* (Desclee, 1996).

Guitton, Jean, *Portrait de Marthe Robin,* (Grasset, 1986).

Manteau-Bonamy, Père Henri-Marie, *Marthe Robin sous la Conduite de Marie,* (St Paul, 1995).

_____Prier 15 Jours avec Marthe Robin, (Nouvelle Cité, 2005).

Pagnoux, Jacques, *Marthe Robin, une Femme d'Espérance,* (Fayard, 1996).

Peyret, Père Raymond. Marthe Robin, *La Croix et la Joie* (Desclee, 1981), [English translation: *The Cross and the Joy,* (Alba House, 1983), currently out of print].

_____Prends Ma Vie Seigneur: La Longue Messe de Marthe Robin, (Desclee, 1985).

_____Petite Vie de Marthe Robin, (Desclee, 1988).

_____Marthe Robin, L'Offrande d'une Vie, (Salvator 2007).

Peyrous, Père Bernard, *Vie de Marthe Robin,* (Emmanuel 2006).

Ravanel, Père Jacques, *Le Secret de Marthe Robin,* (Presses de la Renaissance, 2008).

Tierny, Père Michel, Martin Blake and David Fanning, *Marthe Robin: A Chosen Soul,* (Catholic Truth Society, B652, 1999).

Les Passions de Marthe Robin, (Editions Foyer de Charité, 2009).

Actes Du Colloque, 6-7 juin 2003 à Châteauneuf-de-Galaure.

Alouette. Many articles on Marthe Robin in the Foyer Magazine, (5 issues per year).

Il est Vivant magazine, January 1991, (for Yves de Boisredon testimony).

Appendix

Daily Prayers in the Foyers of Charity

The Angelus

The Angel of the Lord declared unto Mary and she conceived of the Holy Spirit. *Hail Mary....*
Behold the handmaid of the Lord. Be it done unto me according to thy word. *Hail Mary....*
And the Word was made flesh and dwelt amongst us. *Hail Mary....*
Pray for us, O Holy Mother of God; that we may be made worthy of the promises of Christ.
Let us pray: Pour forth, we beseech Thee, O Lord, Thy grace into our hearts, that we to whom the Incarnation of Christ thy Son was made known by the message of an angel, may by his Passion and Cross be brought to the glory of his Resurrection; through the same Christ our Lord. Amen.

Daily Consecration to Mary

I Choose You Today, Mary, in the presence of the angels and saints of heaven, for my Mother and Queen. I consecrate to you, in obedience and love, all that I am, all that I have, and all the good that I may do, putting myself and all that belongs to me entirely at your service, for the greater glory of God in time and in eternity. (St Louis de Montfort)

Prayer to St Joseph

Glorious Saint Joseph, head of the Holy Family of Nazareth, and so zealous in providing for all its needs, extend your tender care over all the Foyers of Charity, their Fathers, their members and their friends. Take under your guidance all their spiritual and temporal needs. And let their end be for the glory of God and the salvation of souls.

Prayer to Our Lady

Beloved Mother, you who know so well the paths of holiness and love, teach us to lift our minds and our hearts often to God, and to fix our respectful and loving attention on the Trinity. And since you walk with us on the path of eternal life, do not remain a stranger to the weak pilgrims your charity is ready to welcome. Turn your merciful face to us. Draw us into your light. Flood us with your kindnesses. Take us into the light and the love. Always take us further and higher into the splendours of heaven. Let nothing ever trouble our peace, nor turn us from the thought of God. But let each minute take us further into the depths of the awesome mystery, till the day when our souls—fully receptive to the light of the divine union—will see all things in eternal love and unity. Amen. (Marthe Robin)

Prayers Composed by Marthe Robin

Anima Christi

O Lord my God, while I am nourished each day by your Sacred Body, washed by your Redeeming Blood, enriched by your Holy Soul, flooded by your Divinity, may I love, desire, search for, wish for, and taste only You. Let my heart and my whole being sigh for You alone, that I may be all yours and concerned only for You; that I may dwell perpetually with You, in You and united to You, in order that I may be entirely consumed in the ardent furnace of your Divine Heart. May I also be united as a child to the Immaculate Heart of my beloved Mother, with whom I want to glorify, praise, serve and obey You for ever.

At Christmas Time

Divine Child Jesus, have pity on people who are all alone; have pity on lonely souls. Take care of them all and gather them to yourself on this evening's Feast, this night of Love, this dawn of peace and hope; so that their pain-filled hearts and troubled minds may find a refuge with their most loving, tender, all-powerful and true friend. If I can feel them huddled near You, O my King, all my sufferings will melt away, forgotten in love. Holy Child of the manger, who bring blessings and joy to the world, come into the souls who await You, who call to You, and make your heavenly dwelling within them, the house of your rest, your blessed manger.

All for the Love of God

Lord, I am ready to receive from your hand a more crushing cross and more lacerating sufferings if that is your will. I want to ransom souls, not with gold or silver, but with the small change of my sufferings united with the inexhaustible treasure of the sufferings of the Redeemer and of his most Holy Mother, by the powerful means of the Cross, which is put at my disposal through the daily offering and silent immolation of my Life to the Creator, who has given it to me. God is my Father, my Brother, and my special Friend, and from the moment that I became his child, his sister and his servant, nothing but nothing at all will happen to me, and I shall have nothing to suffer or undergo and nothing to endure, without as a good Father his having allowed and prepared it in advance.

Any favours obtained through the intercession of Marthe Robin should be reported to: Commission d'Enquête pour la Cause de Marthe Robin, Evêché. BP 825, F 26008 Valence Cedex, France.

For Further Information please contact:

English Friends of the Foyers, St. Mary of the Angels, Moorhouse Road, Bayswater London, W2 5DJ, England. www.foyers.org.uk/ Tel: 020 7229 0487   email: keithbarltrop@rcdow.org.uk

To contact the author, please email: mblake@onetel.com

The English Friends produce a newsletter giving details of Foyer Retreats and other relevant information usually twice a year. To receive a copy by post, please contact the above address. A small donation would be appreciated. To receive the electronic version, please email: foyers@theotokos.org.uk

The address of the Irish Foyer is: "Nazareth," Leperstown Cross, Dunmore East, Co. Waterford, Ireland.
Phone (353) 51 383 383, email: frkilian@eircom.net

In recent years Foyer retreats in English have taken place during the summer at the Foyer at Tressaint in Brittany, France, and also in Britain; these are expected to continue in the future. Such retreats last five days, are held in silence, and usually involve three talks each day. Retreatants also join the community for morning and evening prayer, the Mass, and the Rosary.

Further information from Fr David Hartley at: frdavid@foyers.org.uk   or the Tressaint Foyer at:
Tél : +33 (0)2 96 85 86 00   foyerdecharite@tressaint.com
The Tressaint web site can be seen at: www.tressaint.com

The address of the Courset Foyer is:
19, Rue de Sacriquier, BP 105, 62240, Courset, France.
Phone : +33 (0)3 21 91 62 52   contact@foyer-courset.fr

For further information on the Foyers of Charity worldwide and on Marthe Robin, see: www.foyer-de-charite.com

In the United States see: www.foyerofcharity.com

Theotokos Books Foyer Titles

Christian Living: The Spirituality of the Foyers of Charity

by Donal Anthony Foley
Foreword by Fr Ian Ker

Christian Living: The Spirituality of the Foyers of Charity is based on retreat Conferences at the Foyer of Charity at Courset, near Boulogne in France. It outlines the spirituality of the Foyers and shows that a truly Christian life is possible even in our frenetic world.

This book focuses on how we are all called to discipleship and holiness, to genuinely follow Christ, and how prayer must be an absolute priority in our lives if we are to do God's will. The importance of making time for silence, meditation, and contemplation in our lives is strongly emphasised.

"This slim book, attractively and simply written, gives us the authentic flavor of a Foyer retreat. It will be compulsive reading for anyone fascinated by Marthe Robin, whose spiritual influence on the Church in France can still be felt today, as well as for anyone interested in attending a retreat in one of the Foyers—or even contemplating joining one. And finally, it is ideal spiritual reading for the general reader."
From the foreword by Fr Ian Ker

Donal Anthony Foley has been interested in the Foyers since the 1980's. He has degrees in Humanities and Theology, and has previously written books on Marian apparitions. He has been on numerous Foyer retreats both in England and in France, and has also spent time as a member of the community at several French Foyers.

ISBN 0955074614 - 160pp - £7.95/$11.95/11.95 euros

To order please visit:

www.theotokos.org.uk/pages/books/foyerbook/foyerbook.html

or you can order via online booksellers or through your local bookseller.

Theotokos Books Marian Titles

Marian Apparitions, the Bible, and the Modern World

by Donal Anthony Foley
Foreword by Fr Aidan Nichols OP

Imprimatur from Bishop McMahon of Nottingham, England

ISBN 0852443137 - 374pp - £19.99

This is an in depth investigation into the major Marian apparitions that have occurred during the last five centuries. It relates them to secular happenings and important revolutionary events in Western history including the Reformation and the French and Russian Revolutions. It also argues that the major apparitions are not random or historically inconsequential events, but actually seem to follow a preordained plan, one intimately linked with the biblical Marian typology explored by the Church Fathers. In particular, this books looks at the importance of Fatima in the life of the Church, its links with the papacy, and its continuing relevance for the Third Millennium.

"With his Marian Apparitions, the Bible, and the Modern World, Donal Foley has made a very important contribution to our understanding and appreciation of private revelations, in particular those of Our Lady. ... Not only ... scholars and believers, but the general public will find this volume informative and inspirational."

- Fr. Peter M. Fehlner, F.I.

"Donal Foley has written a book with an extraordinary message."

- Fr Aidan Nichols OP

To order please visit:

www.theotokos.org.uk/pages/books/mariapps/mariapps.html

or: www.amazon.co.uk/exec/obidos/ASIN/0852443137/theotokoscath-21

or you can order via online booksellers or through your local bookseller.

Lightning Source UK Ltd.
Milton Keynes UK
08 February 2011

167133UK00001B/13/P